Women's and Children's Chambers of Parliament

Girls survive on the boyfriend economy, mothers
on the sweat economy, who cares?

Women's and Children's Chambers of Parliament

*Democratizing representation
centuries after Aristotle*

UNITY ELIAS YANG

authorHOUSE®

AuthorHouse™ UK
1663 Liberty Drive
Bloomington, IN 47403 USA
www.authorhouse.co.uk
Phone: 0800.197.4150

Published by AuthorHouse 05/07/2015

ISBN: 978-1-5049-4192-1 (sc)
ISBN: 978-1-5049-4191-4 (hc)
ISBN: 978-1-5049-4193-8 (e)

Print information available on the last page.

Contents

PREFACE

When a housewife described the way that she and the children manage water cuts at home I realized the danger of treating some human activities as secondary to others.

The problems that women have in the society are serious, yet they do not control the systems which are required to solve them. It is important that men understand and accept the fact that no one else can solve a problem better than the person who is suffering from it. Men do not master very well the world that women live in and even when they do, they either ignore it or try to force women to take from them.

Children are either ignored or treated like objects. Their rights are rarely respected or recognized and they are not adequately protected against the harsh conditions of life. Children's problems are not taken seriously by adults who think that children need only the basics of life and not the best.

Creating separate chambers for women and children in parliament will provide an opportunity for specific problems of the two vulnerable groups of human beings to be brought to light at the highest level of the society. After all, it is said that – a problem exposed is half solved.

Men will gain more by living with women and children who are happy, creative and prosperous, than with helpless, desperate and miserable women and children. White people in the United States and in South Africa did not lose part of their human dignity because black people were given their own human dignity. In the same way, men will not lose their power and authority if women are given the appropriate space that they need to live in by their own right.

INTRODUCTION

Women are described as the weaker sex by men because men are always speaking for women and preventing them from speaking for themselves. Children are described as a vulnerable group by adults, who speak for them and control every aspect of their lives.

Speaking for others, experts say, has always been a delicate and controversial issue. After all, it's practically impossible for the speaker to effectively understand and transmit the true feelings of the person he is speaking for. The speaker may belong to a different social group, and he may be speaking about and not speaking for the person he claims to represent.

According to Linda Alcoff in the article: "The Problem of Speaking for Others," there is much discussion going on in anthropology about whether it is possible to adequately or justifiably speak for others. Speaking for others, Alcoff says, has come under increasing criticism; and in some communities it is being rejected. Some feminists' thinking holds that speaking for others is arrogant, vain, unethical, and politically illegitimate.

Speaking for women and children is the norm in most communities. Unfortunately, there is great ignorance about the limits and dangers of blocking women and children from speaking for themselves. The fate of women and children is no different from that of Third World countries when a more powerful group seeks to speak for them.

Linda Alcoff, in the excerpt below, describes the consequences when a person in the developed world is speaking for a person in the Third World. These consequences can be related to the situation where a man, the stronger sex is speaking for a woman, the weaker sex or, an adult (stronger person) is speaking for a child, a weaker person.

"In a situation where a well-meaning First World person is speaking for a person or group in the Third World, the very discursive arrangement may re-inscribe the 'hier- archy of civilizations.' This effect occurs because the speaker is positioned as authoritative and empowered, while the group in the Third World is reduced. As this speaking practice must be championed from afar, this arrangement thus removes any power from the victims. Though the speaker may be trying to materially improve the situation of some lesser-privileged group, the effect of her discourse is to reinforce racist, imperialist conceptions, and perhaps also to further silence the lesser-privileged group's ability to speak and be heard." Source: Cultural Critique, No. 20 (Winter, 1991-1992), pp. 26

The idea for this book developed from an analysis made by one woman in a radio discussion on how a housewife manages water shortage when the taps in a home run dry. She disclosed that whenever the taps went dry, the man of the house at times is not aware, and any existing water reserves in the home is automatically set aside for him. The woman then takes the responsibility to look for alternative sources of water and mobilizes her entire household, except her husband, for an outdoor search for more water.

The complexity of fetching water outside the home is serious. This complexity depends on circumstances like the distance to the source, the quality of the water, the quality of the receptacles and transportation. Most homes, it should be noted, do not often have the recourses to effectively manage such water cuts, which at times go on for days and at times for weeks. Women, she said, are therefore always confronted with such a responsibility, which they may not have the resources needed to manage it. These are responsibilities that society, and especially the men folk, considers to be a woman's business; therefore, it must be easy to accomplish and needs little effort to carry out.

The water shortage crisis is just the tip of an iceberg of complex situations and problems that society (in its present structure) places on women and children, and yet does not give them a voice and the chance to express themselves. This means that, in defining the national policy for domestic water supply and management, the point of view of women and children must take center position; otherwise, the problem will be considered as just one of the many problems on the table of policy managers.

The world of women and that of children is too vast such that man, who plays the role of controller general, does not possess the capacity to exercise full control over them. It is in the interest of men to empower women and the child, and to make them reasonable, responsible and autonomous. By doing so, he will liberate himself from the overbearing role of controller, provider and shock bearer.

Civilization has transformed the ways and means of survival from physical, labor-intensive work to intellectual-intensive work. In the old society, man dominated because he put to use his physical strength to make things to happen. Today, a lot has changed and the increasing use of the brain in doing by far many more things than physical force ever did has opened the way for the modernizing society to reconsider a great part of its old habits.

Human development is the wash word of the modernizing world. It is characterized by training the human brain to be able to see the same things in a different way, and be able to develop and use scientific methods and processes in solving the problems of daily life. Fortunately, for the human system, women and children have brains like men that can be trained to develop and apply scientific processes in solving the problems of daily life.

Men, who still belong to the traditional school of the old system, should not fear that their authority may be eroded by empowering women. The authority of man will increase if he lives and works with people who are empowered. Ignorant and untrained people do not know how-to respect and honor. A well-trained woman is less stubborn and disrespectful than an untrained one. Educated children are easier to manage than uneducated ones. Education and training instills self-control and discipline in those who receive it, and that is the reason why the police will prefer to use education to guide public behavior rather than use the baton to control public indecency.

A second reason why traditional men should not fear to empower their women is this corollary: When black people were subjugated to slavery in the United States of America, and relegated to background citizens in the Republic of South Africa, people of good faith across the world criticized this inexplicable denigration of the human person. The white people who perpetrated slavery and subjugation nurtured fears about the consequence of empowering black people. They could not imagine how they would accommodate emancipated black people in their vicinity. But then slavery eventually stopped in the United States, and apartheid ended in South Africa; and in either case, black people were liberated and empowered.

No evidence exists to my knowledge which shows that the empowerment of black people in the two countries has reduced the authority and power of the white people with whom they share the same country. Black people might have become presidents in both cases, but then not because the white people were prevented from voting or participating. In the case of Barrack Obama, who became the first black President of the United States, the number of votes counted showed that more white people than black people voted for him.

Fear by traditionalists that an empowered woman is a threat to man's authority and power is a negative and regressive worry, which will only prolong abuse to women and children and general human suffering. The problems of human society are many, and gender domination and rivalry has not provided a way forward over the centuries.

It is important to make this appeal to men: As our eyes cannot ignore the beauty of our women, our ears should not ignore the cries of their suffering and neglect. The alarming plight and suffering of our women has been around for centuries. Millions of women across the world complain that men and society does not give them the chance to solve problems.

Changing the fate of our women will require several stages of action, which to me must begin by giving women the chance to begin to speak for themselves. Our mothers, sisters, daughters, and wives should speak about the pain of childbearing and upbringing, early marriage, female genital mutilation, widowhood, divorce, abortion, cultural discrimination and restrictions, joblessness and poverty, male domination, brutality, etc.

Women, it should be carefully noted, are not innocent of their plight because men are in no way the sole cause of their tragic situation. Women do contribute immensely to the suffering they undergo. In many societies, the socio-cultural environment in which the young woman grows corrupts her mindset and creates an entirely unrealistic picture of how the society works. The gender conflict picks its roots when the young woman begins to inculcate the feeling of dependency on man instead of collaboration. It's a situation that embarrasses and frustrates the spirit of the young man, who intends to withstand the inevitable pressure emanating from the woman. This creates the free rider/taxpayer discrepancy and inequality. That is how the gender conflict kicks off and metamorphosis from one stage to another and from one level to another.

The child's world is even more complex and delicate than that of the woman. Different from an adult in almost every aspect, the child unfortunately is completely dependent on adults, and the two have little or nothing in common. How do children solve their problems? Are adults aware of children's problems? If the answer is yes, to what level do adults master and participate in solving such problems? Adults are very proud people. After all, when an adult describes something as childish, the implication is that it is valueless, foolish and only good to be thrown out. Childish is therefore the way adults describe and perceive everything that comes from the child. With this preconceived perception of the child by adults, the consequence is clear; the child's world is simply ignored by adults, and the adult's world is imposed on the child.

Children's problems can fall within three categories: physical, psychological and sexual. Physical problems of children deal with the environment in which he/she lives and the material needs of life. This is where adults intervene most, creating the impression that they are taking full care of the problems that children face. Psychological problems touch on the state of mind of children on issues like fear of danger, separation from parents, desire for specific toys or objects, and worries about the future. These are ignored by adults. Sexuality problems relate to the sexual sentiments of the child, which comes to play from birth and metamorphosis with age. This is the most ignored of the three problems, as adults generally treat sexuality as a taboo.

To conclude, this book does not speak for women and children, it appeals to society to help our women to achieve their full potential in society. And our goal is to make them become more independent and useful to themselves and to society in general. Give women the opportunity to speak for themselves, and we shall know better who they are and what they want. It is said that a problem shared is half solved. Give women and children a forum to speak for themselves and their problems will be half solved, and society will enjoy more peace and progress.

CHAPTER 1

The Problem

When I started writing this book, my initial view of women, and the world in which they live, was one of pity for a group of people I thought did not see anything wrong with the profile of their lives. I felt that women did not know what to do about their present fate, that they were victims of both their ignorance and destiny. In fact, I thought that destiny had designed them to be as such, and had prepared them to accept it as such.

It was not until I was going through Peter Watson's book, "A Terrible Beauty," that I came across the enigmatic Simone de Beauvoir and her big book, "The Second Sex," which was first published in 1949.

Simone de Beauvoir, I call her a tiger, for she may not be at ease with the appellation of tigress, and her book did not only answer the question I had about what women think of themselves, but also presented a complete analysis about the origin, causes and way out of women's present dilemma, in a society which they feel has been confiscated and dominated by man.

The biological, historical, cultural, social, economic and political arguments that Beauvoir raises in "The Second Sex," tell the full story of women. She reveals that "One is not born, but rather becomes, a woman." She goes on to raise highly researched, intelligent and related socio-cultural and scientific facts to back up the hypothesis. In her study of biology, psychoanalysis, and historical materialism, she came across the glaring differences that exist between men and women, but did not find any justification to women's so-called inferiority.

Beauvoir is right to blame the present situation of women on society and on the male sex in particular. She is right because, the present human order defined by its culture and civilization has been designed completely by humans. Apart from creating life and death, and the environment to accommodate it, nothing else relating to our life style was decreed by the Creator.

Asked whether he believed in God, a captain from the Biafra region of Nigeria under the captivity of the Federal Army during the Nigerian Civil War replied: He knows that God created the universe and gave it systemic rules on how it will work, and allowed it to itself. In other words, immediately after the universe came into being, its maker abandoned it to itself, but not without imposing on it the law of nature or creation.

In some form of affirming the captain's philosophy about God, Simone de Beauvoir throughout her analysis does not blame God and nature for putting women in their present dilemma. Not at all! That is why she declares that one is not born, but rather becomes, a woman.

There is no convincing evidence to show that nature and not man has shaped the present world order. Man has been on the front seat steering the path that humanity is following, and today we are where we are because of man. It is easy to find evidence to prove that man is the one who is shaping the things in our world; for example, the great theories that have shaped the human system that are embedded in culture, science, philosophy, economics and politics have being designed by man.

With regards to who is responsible for the processes, that have brought women to the present quagmire, de Beauvoir is categorical and just: men and women are both responsible. She explains that in the pre-Stone Age before the discovery of bronze and the eventual invention of the machete and the hammer, both men and women were equals in every aspect.

This was so because the physical force of man, without the support of tools, could not pull down the forest trees, nor combat the wild animals. In this circumstance, man was not very different from woman. The two therefore lived as equals because man had nothing special to show that made him look very different from woman.

It appears things started taking a new turn, and male domination of the female saw the light of day, when the metal called bronze came into play. Using bronze, man invented the lance to clear bushes and cut down trees, the arrow to hit wild animals, the hammer to fabricate new tools, etc.

In her heavily researched analysis, de Beauvoir cited Gaston Bachelard's description of the influence of the blacksmith's inventions on man's road to domination; and she concludes by blaming the advent of male domination of both nature and woman on the invention of these basic tools.

Before the discovery of bronze and the invention of the machete and hammer, one can imagine that man was an idle person, having little work to do. The absence of tools reduced man to collector of fruits and maybe dead animals as food subsistence for his family.

The function of collecting, instead of cultivating food, according to de Beauvoir, signified a period of undisputable equality between man and women because man's rule was not extraordinary and did not make him look special or different from woman. Both were exposed and vulnerable, and suffered the same brutality from the violent jungle of wild vegetation and animals.

It appears rather that it was woman and her responsibility of maternity that played a difficult and complicated role, and not man, during this period. The procedure of child conception, delivery and upbringing in the woman has never changed since creation; the pain, and the stress have remained over the centuries. Science and technology have done little to reduce the problems that woman faces during maternity. On the contrary, science and technology has greatly reduced the burden of man's manual labor. Hard, physical labor is gradually disappearing, and man's role is becoming increasingly assisted by machines. Before the hammer and the machete were invented, man was less busy. The invention of these primitive tools increased man's range of activities and the means for executing them.

From the age of the primitive tools developed the new man, who was going to use the newfound tools to transform his role from a mere fruit collector to a conqueror of nature and women. Also, over the centuries, man designed and developed the arts of culture, socialization and politics, which gradually shaped the way human beings, perceive nature and the two sexes of mankind. Culture, in particular, has shaped the way man perceives woman and imposed upon her a background role, thereby resulting in the domination of man over woman.

Domination in human systems it should be noted is not limited to man dominating woman only. There are many instances in history where man the male has dominated, tortured and enslaved other males. In the era of barbaric monarchies and satanic tyrannies, men who attempted to oppose existing authorities were mercilessly punished or simply eliminated. One cannot imagine, for example, that concepts such as democracy, human rights and freedom, civil liberties that emerged many hundreds of years ago are still not fully practiced in many societies. Because some class that claim to be upper, feels that it must stay above and dictate to others they consider lower. And the so-called suppressed lower class is made up of both men and women.

In racial conflicts throughout history, one particular race, for reasons known only to its members, will unilaterally declares its supremacy over other races and takes measures to enforce such a claim. The alleged superiority of the German race over all others in Europe and elsewhere, has never been backed up with any scientific evidence, nor has the superiority of the white race over black been demonstrated. Scientific evidence produced by white researchers has proved instead that the black skin is superior and healthier to the white skin.

In India, where the cast system is still practiced, attempts by some members of the upper cast to prove their domination of the lower cast, are manifested on near daily basis. It is accomplished through degrading acts like rape orchestrated by men from the upper cast on girls from the lower, with the intention to humiliate not only the women, but also the men who are either the fathers, brothers, boyfriends and husbands of the women they rape. During warfare, combatants are known to have used rape as a weapon against the enemy, as they are aware that one good way to denigrate and torment a man psychologically is to make him know that you had sexual intercourse with his wife or daughter.

In the field of democracy, it is hard to understand that five centuries after Aristotle and others projected its usefulness to humanity, but many societies around the world are still reticent to accept it. And wherever there is no democracy, both men and women are suppressed and misruled. The obstruction to democracy has always been a game played by the privileged class who fear that power will be snatched from them by the proletariat. The ruling class understands the trick better than the deprived masses that political power opens the way to all other forms of power; so, why let it go, to the dogs?

It goes beyond every reasonable doubt that the past and present situation of women has been perpetuated purely by man in the way that he has shaped and made culture and politics to evolve. Like in the conflict between the black and the white race, where science has ruled that black skin is healthier and superior to white skin; in the sex conflict between man and woman, biology has shown that woman is more complex and complicated than man. Here, someone should explain how something that is complex and complicated can be inferior to that which is simple?

History has failed to tell us when, and who, appointed men to take precedence over women. Before the Holy Bible was written hundreds of thousands of years after humanity came into existence, men had already gained sovereignty over women. According to de Beauvoir's, even Freud declared his ignorance about the origins of male sovereignty, but suggests that the sovereignty of the father was a fact of social origin.

Male sovereignty over female therefore might have originated from man's soft spot and love for woman, necessitated by the cruelty of the jungle in which the early man, our ancestor, lived. For fear of extinction of the species by the brutality of bush life, man might have seen it as a necessity to protect woman and child by preserving them in some save hideout, and venturing into the jungle alone. This came with the supposition that if he perishes in the fangs of a wild animal, the woman and child would still survive in their hideout.

The coming of metal tools simple facilitated man's desire to protect women and children from the hungry beasts of the forest, which they unavoidably shared together. Man unilaterally took over command of women as a result of prevailing circumstances. Women freely accepted men's command certainly not because they felt inferior to them, but probably because they realized that man's leadership was producing useful results for her. Man's rise to supremacy over women cannot be differentiated from a society leader's rise to prominence because he started the struggle, or took the frontline in a movement or ideology. After all, to start is to lead, and so, man started and rose to sovereignty.

Man simply took the frontline in protecting the species and became leader. It is not said and proved anywhere that leaders rule over inferior members. The British people are not inferior because they are ruled by the Queen, nor are American citizens inferior to their all powerful President. So, women are not inferior because they are ruled by man. They are not even a second-class citizen.

As English legal experts put it, practice makes a rule, which means that any practice in human systems that is repeated on regular basis (that is not contested by either the actor or the audience), can be a basis for custom and law.

Man's rule over women has reigned for perhaps thousands or millions years, making one suspect that it is the oldest practice in human history and every other custom, culture, religion and philosophy came after it. This probably explains why no custom, culture and religion were able to contradict the practice; they all opted to conform to it. To de Beauvoir, conformity was normal after all, because, man created custom, culture, religion and philosophy without consulting women.

She goes on to accuse religion, philosophy and science written by man for distorting the true intention of God, the Creator, when they define the place of women to be secondary. The Holy Bible, she thinks has not helped women's course by opining that women were made from a part that was extracted from the male's body.

To her such an assertion makes man feel that a woman is only a small portion of the man, the giant when she said, "Legislators, priests, philosophers, writers and scientists have striven to show that the subordinate position of woman is willed in heaven and advantageous on earth. The religions invented by men reflect this wish for domination … they have made use of philosophy… Quotations of Aristotle and St. Thomas … Since ancient times, satirists have delighted in showing up the weaknesses of women." Roman law, while limiting the rights of women, she said simply cited "the imbecility and instability of the sex." She accuses men of trying to make their supremacy a right and cited Poulain de la Barre who said, "Being men, those who have made and compiled the laws have favored their own sex, and jurists have elevated these laws into principles."

Perceptions like this have been at the origin of the sexual conflict, which Beauvoir thinks is baseless and is inspired by ignorance. She uses biological facts to explain that males and females are rather variations on a common groundwork, much as the two gametes are differentiated from similar original tissue. She alerts man that in some species like the praying mantis, after copulation and fertilization, the female kills the male and eats the body; meanwhile in bees, the male serves no useful purpose after it fertilizes the egg.

Today, our strength and capacities are judged from what we do, and not from what we can do. Because man has been doing physically hard things for a long time, and woman has concentrated on childbearing and upbringing, society through culture has been tempted to conclude that it was so ordained (by whom, nobody can say). Freud declared that he does not know who appointed man to lead.

Man's uncontrolled leadership for centuries over women, has placed women in a dilemma; they feel stressed by the system, but then, they do not have what it takes to correct it (power). Beauvoir opines that all the improvement that has occurred in favor of women's rights occurred in areas where men decided to grant such rights to women, and that women did not take them by their own desire and force.

The man-dominated world is still alive and strong, despite the enormous technological evolution that has taken place and has made life easier for humanity; man still does not allow women to leave or add new roles to their historic role. "Notions of femininity, almost without exception, originated in man: man defines the 'eternal feminine'; man insists on female mediocrity; man chains his wife to the hearth. Women, who have no voice, cannot be the 'problem,' just as the 'problem' of Jews and blacks is one invented and perpetuated by their oppressors," de Beauvoir said. Man wants to have all for himself. In some communities for example, man has continued to bar woman from driving a car.

Simone de Beauvoir discloses that man has never questioned his rights in this world, and that conservative bourgeoisie still see in the emancipation of women a menace to their morality and their interests. "Some men," she states, "dread feminine competition ... few of them really wish in their hearts for woman to succeed in making it; those among them who hold woman in contempt see in the sacrifice nothing for them to gain; those who cherish her see too much that they would lose." She quoted a male student who wrote, "Every woman student who goes into medicine or law robs us of a job."

Women like Poulain de la Barre, have accused men for being judge and party in the sex conflict. Such women feel that men are proud and arrogant because they think that they are superior to women as manifested in the Jewish prayer where, men thank God for making them men and not women. "Blessed be God ... that he did not make me a woman." This can be dangerous for any species that wants to be preserved. If all were men, how would the species have survived? Demoralizing a whole segment of the species is equivalent to species suicide.

Denigration of woman by man takes several forms in indifferent communities and cultures. Simone de Beauvoir in "The Second Sex," highlights numerous citations representing man's contempt of women: Aristotle, "The female is a female by virtue of a certain lack of qualities ... we should regard the female nature as afflicted with a natural defectiveness." To St. Thomas, a woman is an imperfect man or simply an "incidental" being. In the book of Genesis in the Bible, Beauvoir complains that, Eve, the woman, has been depicted as made from a bone of Adam, the male.

It's a practice started by man in all honesty, with the sole aim to provide security and preserve the species. It has for over the years transformed his very perception and understanding of nature. Over the centuries, the evolution of man's leadership role has created one big misunderstanding - man feels that he is superior to woman, and woman feels helpless in the fix. The consequences of this dichotomy between men and women are many and weighing on women heavily.

Describing the consequences of the manmade world on women, de Beauvoir says, "Woman is not born fully formed; she is gradually shaped by her upbringing. Biology does not determine what makes a woman a woman—a woman learns her role from man and others in society. A woman is not born passive, secondary, and nonessential, but all the forces in the external world have conspired to make her so."

Irresponsibility of women, which some women take for as a privilege, is another consequence of man's rule, de Beauvoir elucidates without any favors, "Women rely on men for shelter, sustenance, opinions, hobbies, conversation topics—in short, for a reason to live. Making no economic contributions to their household, they spend their lives engaged in useless, repetitive activities."

She raises the blame that, "women fear departing from societal norms and venturing into the wilderness of liberty." And that, "It is less demanding and less exhausting to abdicate all responsibility for one's future to a man," and as a result, "Many women refuse the opportunities granted them; these women will discover that the 'privilege' of irresponsibility is actually a curse, in love and in life." Because, she added, "Any successful relationship between two parties grows from mutual liberty. Irresponsibility is a function of mutilation and incompleteness, of dependency and enslavement." She goes on to declare that, "Women are 'clinging', they are a dead weight, and they suffer for it; the point is that their situation is like that of a parasite sucking out the living strength of another organism."

In an overview of "The Second Sex," the writer discloses that every force in society conspires to deprive women of subjectivity and flatten them into objects. They are denied the possibility of independent work or creative fulfillment, and must accept a dissatisfying life of housework, childbearing, and sexual slavishness. He claims that, a bourgeois woman performs three major functions of; wife, mother, and entertainer, and no matter how illustrious the woman's household maybe, these roles inevitably lead to incompleteness, and frustration. He cites Beauvoir and concluded that, the woman's situation is *not* a result of her character, but rather, her character is a result of her situation. "Woman's mediocrity, complacency, lack of accomplishment, laziness, passivity" he wrote, "are the *consequences* of her subordination, not the cause."

Simone de Beauvoir, in "The Second Sex" makes very bold and far-reaching proposals as to the way forward for the recreation of woman. She suggests that women should be provided with living strength of their own, by letting them to have the means to attack the world and wrest from it their own subsistence; and as such, their dependence will be abolished and that of man as well. "There is no doubt that both men and women will profit greatly from the new situation," she declares.

In an indebt confrontation between nature and culture, she opines that erotic liberty should be recognized by custom, but the sexual act should not be considered a "service" to be paid for. That women should be obliged to provide themselves with other ways of earning a living, and marriage should be based on a free agreement that the contracting parties could break at will.

Challenging the socio-political and legal dispensation, she recommends that maternity should be voluntary, and contraception and abortion be authorized. All mothers and their children she said "were to have exactly the same rights, in or out of marriage; pregnancy leaves were to be paid for by the state, which would assume charge of the children, signifying not that they would be taken away from their parents, but that they would not be abandoned to them."

According to Beauvoir, the upbringing of girls needs to be fixed. If little girls were brought up from the first with the same demands and rewards, the same severity and the same freedom, as their brothers, taking part in the same studies, the same games, promised the same future, surrounded with women and men who seemed to her undoubted equals, the meanings of sexual inequality would be profoundly modified. She explains that if the mother assumes on the same basis as the father the material and moral responsibility of the marriage, the mother would enjoy the same lasting prestige and the child would perceive around her an equal world and not a masculine world.

Insisting on the need to reconsider the way boys and girls are trained, she states, "authorized to test her powers in work and sports, competing actively with the boys, she would not find the absence of the penis – compensated by the promise of a child, enough to give rise to an inferiority complex; correlatively, the boy would not have a superiority complex if it were not instilled into him and if he looked up to women with as much respect as to men."

If equality is practiced in the upbringing of the boy and the girl child, Beauvoir thinks, "the little girl would not seek sterile compensation in narcissism and dreaming, she would not take her fate for granted; she would be interested in what she was doing; she would throw herself without reserve into undertakings."

She warns that, it would be beneficial above all for the young girl not to be influenced against taking charge herself of her own existence, for then she would not seek a demigod in the male, but a comrade, a friend, and a partner. Alerting anyway that her intention is not, of course, to wave aside with the back of the hand, all the difficulties that the child has to overcome in changing into an adult; she states that, "The most intelligent and tolerant of education could not relieve the child of experiencing things for herself; what could be asked is that obstacles should not be piled gratuitously in her path."

As to what hopes exist in the horizon for the advancement of women's struggle for equality and liberation, de Beauvoir had this, "If a caste is kept in a state of inferiority, no doubt it remains inferior; but liberty can break the circle. Let the Negroes vote and they become worthy of having the vote; let woman be given responsibilities and she is able to assume them."

To her, oppressors cannot be expected to make a move of gratuitous generosity; that is, man liberating women by his own will, but at one time, the revolt of the oppressed, and at another time the very evolution of the privileged caste itself, will create new situations that will cause or create the desired liberation. She feels that, so far, men have been led, in their own interests, to give partial emancipation to women.

Women should therefore continue their ascent, and the successes they are obtaining are an encouragement for them to do so. And if women could sooner or later, arrive at complete economic and social equality, then, an inner metamorphosis would occur. Citing the influence of technological expansion, de Beauvoir foresees the eventual collapse of male domination, "Technology" she said, "being the power of the brain and not of the brawn – the male rationale that women are the weaker sex and hence must play a secondary role, can no longer be logically maintained."

Simone de Beauvoir recognized and encouraged the current evolution and changes that are taking place in favor of women's struggle. In an interview she granted John Gerassi of "The Society" in 1976, she remarked that a positive change is taking place among women, especially through the activities of feminist movements when she said that, when she was 25, "Among even the most intimate of my women friends then, truly feminine problems were never discussed. Now, because of consciousness groups and the toughness of the desire to genuinely confront women's problems within these groups, real friendships among women have developed. In the past, women tended never to become genuine friends with other women. They saw each other as rivals, enemies, or competitors. Now, not only are women capable of being true friends, they have learned to be warm, open, and deeply tender with each other."

Thanks to feminist groups, many women are now capable of saying openly that they are lesbian, a situation that was unthinkable in the past. This was a breakthrough according to de Beauvoir, but much is still to be done in the bringing in women from all classes of society. Women are not yet collected to face the problem; most of them are still tied to class values and norms. This can be verified because the women waging the fight for liberation are mostly bourgeois intellectuals; workers' wives and even female workers remain firmly attached to the society's middle-class value system.

According to one analyses of de Beauvoir's work, the fear by some women of breaking societal norms and venturing into an unknown freedom is the main obstacle to the feminine struggle; "the difficulty of breaking free from 'femininity' —of sacrificing security and comfort for some ill-conceived notion of 'equality' —induces many women to accept the usual unfulfilling roles of wife and mother."

The economic situation of women is highlighted as the main source of feminine subjugation. Simone de Beauvoir discloses that economic underpinnings of being female is the cause of her subordination, and that her liberation will lie in her economic roots. "Only in work can she achieve autonomy." To her, if a woman can support herself, she can also achieve a form of liberation.

As a realist myself, throughout my exploration of the work of Simone de Beauvoir, *a tiger,* by my rating, I have come across very little, or no clear area of disagreement with all the arguments she raised. Her ideas came in direct reinforcement and enrichment to mine. I take delight to conclude this chapter, which cropped up from her book and which I dedicate to her, with the following revelations by her. And that to me, summaries the woman problem and is necessary to spark off the reflection, which is required to push our women out of the present trap.

She thinks that to emancipate woman is to refuse to confine her to the relations she bears to man, not to deny them to her. Let woman have her independent existence and she will continue nonetheless to exist for man. If the two sexes can mutually recognize each other as subject, each will remain for the other. The reciprocity of their relations will not do away with miracles such as desire, possession, love, dreams, and adventure, created by the divisions of human beings into two separate categories; and the words that move us such as: giving, conquering, and uniting, will not lose their meaning. On the contrary, when we abolish the slavery of half of humanity, with the whole system of hypocrisy that it implies, then the "division" of humanity will reveal its genuine significance and the human couple will find its true form.

"It is not a question of abolishing in woman the contingencies and miseries of the human condition, but of giving her the means for transcending them." Simone de Beauvoir.

CHAPTER 2

Representation and Parliament

In real life, human beings interact with one another through intensive and complex relationships. The battle for survival has imposed an unavoidable interdependence whereby everyone of us will need assistance of some form from the others.

Humans therefore interact with one another because they need assistance from one another. Relationships that result from interactions by people are governed by a science called politics, which according to Aristotle is the queen of the sciences. To Herbert Spiro, it is through politics that humanity shall develop or destroy itself.

Unfortunately, many people still limit politics to partisan or party politics and fall short to understand and appreciate its extended forms in all sectors of the human system. Aristotle defines politics as the queen of the sciences; a straightforward way to describe the place of politics in the life of every human system.

Herbert Spiro warns humanity that it is through politics that the human system will develop or be destroyed, which means that politics is at the center of all human activities, it influences and is influenced by all actions human beings take. This can be related as follows:

The bomb invented by science is used to kill human beings during a war caused by a dispute on the waters of a river used in irrigating farmland. Through such disputes and wars, Spiro warns, humanity can destroy itself.

The ambulance invented by science is used to rush a seriously ill person to the hospital where his life is saved and he returns to continue working for his community. Through such social welfare schemes, humanity shall develop and be preserved according to Spiro.

To help human beings to manage their daily relationships and interests, politics has devised a tool called representation or political representation, which is the of this book, that enables each one of us to participate directly or better still indirectly in orientating our interactions with one another. Political philosophers and engineers have all agreed that it may not be as good a tool as polity. In 1762, Rousseau in *Of the Social Contract,* likens representation to the use of mercenary soldiers. To him, the moral capacity of persons and the soul of politics cannot be delegated. He affirms that, "Sovereignty cannot be represented for the same reason that it cannot alienated; it consists essentially in the general will, and the will does not admit of being represented." However, practice has shown that representation is the minimum acceptable workable option for the management of human systems.

Polity or direct participation experimented by the Greeks in the 5th century required everyone to take part in the day-to-day management of the society in what is known as government by the people for the people. Everyone was expected to be present in the village square assemblies, where decisions were taken concerning the interest of the community.

Polity did not operate for a long time because not everyone could be present for the village square assembly all the time for the diverse reasons that anyone can imagine. The imperatives of government by the people, for the people, required that a more practical model be put in place to take care of the interests of everyone.

Representation or indirect participation emerged as the acceptable option, despite its limits and weaknesses. Over the centuries, representation has shaped the way human systems are governed across the world leading to the birth of institutions like local councils, regional or provincial councils and parliaments.

What is representation? Represent in other words means to present again, that is, re-present someone or something. According to Hanna Pitkin in *The Concept of Representation,* represent simply means to make present again. A parent who seeks admission for his 5-year-old son in a kindergarten represents him to the school authority. In political representation, the representative simply presents or makes present the constituents again. For example, when a member of parliament sits in the assembly, he is seen to be carrying on him the people of his constituency.

Several forms of representation take place in daily life; it can be in the form of a parent representing his child, a family member acting on behalf of relatives, an association representing its members and otherwise, or an institution representing those it was created to protect or control. Representation can take place with or without the consent of the represented. This book will focus on representation with consent carried out by licensed institutions such as local and regional councils, as well as parliaments.

Local and regional councils and modern parliaments have been put in place to carry out the function that the village square assembly of ancient Greece attempted to perform. The early forms of parliament were heavily undemocratic and were conceived and designed to help the ruler to govern his subjects. That was the case with the Sicilian, Icelandic and Faroes Parliaments which are believed to be among the first parliaments in the world.

The modern parliament on the contrary, is elected directly by the people to protect their interest. The word parliament or *parlement* was first used in 1236 by the French- speaking noble class in England. The word comes from the French word *parler,* which means to "talk."

This is probably the reason why the English Parliament is the oldest in the world and seen to be the mother of modern parliaments. Its roots took off in the 13th century with the Curia Regis the king's feudal council, and evolved to become the House of Lords, which is today the Upper House of the British Parliament.

A second chamber of the British Parliament called the House of Commons later developed as a result of persistent conflict between the king and his barons. The House of Lords and the House of Commons have evolved over the centuries to become the longest surviving bicameral parliament in the world.

Bicameral parliament is a system whereby, the institution of parliament is made up of two separate chambers or houses, one of them defined as the lower house and the other as the upper house. Most upper houses are called the senate. Most countries run bicameral parliaments; others maintain a single-house chamber.

What is most interesting here is the fact that parliament has evolved from an undemocratic powerless institution, initially serving the interest of rulers and the barons, to becoming a democratic, representative and powerful institution serving the interest of common men and women in the different systems of government, be they presidential, parliamentary, semi-presidential or parliamentary systems.

In a presidential system of government, there is a sharp separation of powers between the executive and the legislature branches. The head of the executive is generally very powerful exercising some executive prerogative that may escape the control of the legislature. Examples of presidential systems of government include: the United States, Russia, Nigeria, South Africa, Afghanistan, Brazil, Benin, Guyana, South Korea, etc.

A parliamentary system of government is one where the head of the executive comes from parliament and is controlled by it. The head of the executive here is like a child of parliament, who is assigned to manage the executive in collaboration with parliament and reporting to it. Parliamentary control is the order of the day. The British system of government is the longest surviving parliamentary system in the world and others include: Canada, India, Australia, Jamaica and Japan.

Semi-presidential or parliamentary system of government is simply one that is half presidential and half parliamentary. This means that power shuffles between the executive and the legislature and is effectively shared between a powerful president who is the head of state, head of the executive and a powerful prime minister, who is the head of government and an agent of parliament. Here, executive power is split between a president, who is elected by universal suffrage, and a prime minister, who is appointed from the party with the majority seats in parliament. Examples of semi-presidential or parliamentary systems of government include: France, Peru, Taiwan, Cameroon, etc.

Is representation necessary? The answer to this question resides in the failure of polity or direct representation. Man, by nature, will always desire and ask for the best in life; but unfortunately he does not always receive the best, and that is why initial attempts to run a government through the direct participation by all citizens never worked and the system of indirect participation, which was initially rejected, became the cornerstone in participative government.

The purposes of representation are to enable everyone to participate in government, and to give the government in power legitimacy. To rule over anyone, a ruler must have connections with the ruled. That is, there must exist a line linking the one to the other with each one of them able to identify the other. The ruled or citizens must be able to clearly recognize the institutions of leadership, and identify with the people who head such institutions at any given time. The ruler or institutions of leadership must in return be able to demonstrate a mastery of their constituents, either in person or as an inhabitant of a territory over his jurisdiction.

Representation therefore serves as a form of division of labor between the governed and the governor, whereby, the governed authorizes the governor to rule so as to give the governed time enough to carry out other activities related to his personal life or to the life of his society. The governor on his part solicits the collaboration of the governed in the realization of the activities of government.

The division of labor between the governed and the governor through political representation has come to stay as the most pragmatic arrangement between the always busy governed or represented, and the governor or representative. Every individual uses more than 90 percent of his energy on personal activities and the doubt is less that many will not dispose the energy to always attend a village square government meeting.

With much energy dedicated to personal activities, the represented will appear at times to be cut off from the representative who intend will appear to be acting without the consent of the represented. In economic life, division of labor works out well because each labor actor works for his personal interest to realize the objective of the industry, which is to make profit. In political life, the division of labor between its labor actors, represented and representative, does not work out smoothly because of conflicting interests - the interest of the represented is purely personal and private, while that of the representative is essentially general.

The importance of government in the lives of individuals has been on the increase over the centuries, as government has shifted from being the ruler's property and instrument of rule and domination of the individual, to become an instrument of facilitation and service provider for the individual.

Modern government serves as protector and provider for the governed and the best only way to accomplish this responsibility is to establish the governor/governed alliance. In this alliance, the governor seeks authorization to govern from the governed through established democratic processes such as elections and referendums.

Once the governor receives the authorization to govern from the governed, it transforms such authorization into powers, which it then uses to carry out the complex activity of governing.

In the bygone era of the monarchy, the governed were called subjects of the monarch synonymous to objects or property of the monarch. With the demise of the monarchy, and the emergence of the republic, the governed was upgraded from the status of subject to citizen.

The important difference between a citizen and a subject is centered on the word consent. Subjects were ruled over without their authorization or consent. The ruler enjoyed absolute authority over the subject, who did not have the right even to complain. The ruler who was an absolute monarch represented the subject without his authorization; thereby, constituting forced or undemocratic representation.

Today, the valorization of the human person through the evolution of human rights and human development processes, has replaced subject with citizen. By the new definition, a citizen is a free person, not the property of anyone, and no one shall rule over him without his consent.

Consent of the represented has emerged as the watch word for political representation in a democratic environment. It is acquired through the line of connection or the link that must exist between the representative and the represented; and from it two important orders arise, which are placed on the shoulders of the representative: authorization and accountability. Authorization to represent the represented is acquired automatically once his consent is obtained and the representative can then act on behalf and in the interest of the represented. Representation without authorization is dictatorship.

Accountability requires that the representative should give a loyal report to the represented concerning all the actions taken by the representative on the behalf and interest of the represented. The represented must not be a tool for exploitation by the representative, which is why accountability is the consideration that the represented receives from his representative.

How does a representative get the consent to represent the represented? The method of giving consent will depend on the subject to be represented, which could be: an individual, a friend, a family member, an association, or a population. Considering the fact that the pattern of representation has many similarities for the different subjects that may be represented, it is also possible to deduce how consent may be acquired from Hanna Pitkin's classification of representation into: formalistic, substantive, descriptive and symbolic representation. For the purposes of this book, we shall consider the acquisition of consent to represent a population, which to me fits with Pitkin's formalistic representation, even though, elements of the four types of representation can be depicted irrespective of the subject that is being represented.

A parent is authorized to represent his child because he takes full responsibility over the child; a teacher is authorized to represent a pupil who is registered in his school because of the arrangement between the school and the pupil. Who gives authorization to the mayor and local government, the governor and regional government, and the president and national government to represent the people in their respective territories?

Government emerged as the manager of general interest, which is considered to be area of interest where all or the majority of individual interests intercept. For example, when an individual leaves his private home, he goes out using a public road on which he meets other individuals. The road is the area where the interests of the different individuals intercept and appear to be similar. That's where the government intervenes and provides a road to serve individual, but similar interests.

If the government is around it is because it has some work to do. What is interesting is that government does not have its own interest; it rather has the common interest of its people to promote and protect. This is frequently referred to as general interest.

Government, be it local, regional or national, has a similar responsibility to the population living within their territory in the same way that the parent has responsibility over his child, and the teacher over his students. Government therefore behaves as the representative of general interest and needs to get the consent of its population in order to represent them.

To make it look more representative, govern subdivides itself into an executive, legislative and judiciary wings. The executive and the legislature exercise public power and authority, and are considered as the institutions that represent the population; and in any democratic setup, the head of the executive and all the members of the legislature receive the consent of the population that they represent through free, fair and transparent elections.

Democratic election is therefore the primary way that a population gives its consent to the people and institutions that represent them in government. Through elections, government institutions and their leaders acquire the consent of the masses and therefore the authorization to represent and rule them. To be re-elected in the next elections, representatives in the executive and legislature must be accountable to the people they are representing. Accountability is the only platform on which the represented can control the representative and be able to punish or reward them in the next elections.

Legislative representation is the interest of this book; it will therefore be important for us to make some inroads into the role of parliament as a representing institution. What is parliament and what role does it play in representation?

Parliament is an institution that represents the people of a given area, region or territory in the business of government; it is made up of members or representatives elected from the different communities or groups that make up the area, region or territory.

The group of councilors elected to a council or local government area, constitute a local parliament with representative prerogative to make decisions related to local realities under the guidance and control of higher institutions and authorities. Councilors therefore represent the population in the council or local government area under their electoral constituency.

Regional councilors or delegates are elected to represent the interest of the region or state. They constitute a provincial or regional council or better still state legislature with the prerogative to make regional legislation and control the regional executive. Regional councilors or legislators represent the population that is living in their territory, and their legislative and control powers are limited by the national or central constitution.

National parliament or the legislature is the highest level of democratic political representation. Parliament exists in all, if not most, of the countries around the world even in undemocratic systems of government; there is always a structure that is shaped to look like a parliament. This means that even autocratic and dictatorial regimes find it difficult to rule without an institution that looks like a parliament.

Modern parliaments are purely democratic and are seen to be the apex of representation. Members who seat in the lower house of most parliaments are said to individually represent the entire nation, and not only the constituency that elected them.

What is the role of parliament? Generally, besides the emblematic role of making present again the population in decision making, parliament has regular activities it carries out in the day-to-day running of the state. Parliamentary activities include: making laws and controlling the executive branch of government.

The responsibility of making laws for any country lies with the parliament. Human systems are run by laws which are formulated to reflect the expectations of the society while taking into consideration the diversity of peoples and cultures. The executive arm of government runs the nation using laws made by parliament.

Parliament controls the executive to make sure that it carries out government work in the interest of the population, while respecting laws and norms that project and promote human development. The responsibility of the executive as the day-to-day manager of government and the country is so complex that parliament tries to play the role of a watchdog. It does so by helping the executive to remain focused and disciplined as it pilots the statecraft through the turbulent skies of progress and development.

CHAPTER 3

Democratizing Representation

Has representation evolved from a unilaterally imposed concept to a democratic one, after it imposed itself as the minimum acceptable method where everyone in the society can participate in decision making and government?

Who is representing who, where and for what? Answering this question brings to the limelight lots of other unanswered questions. After the failure of polity in the 5th century, it is unimaginable how long it has taken mankind to get to the present level of democratization.

To answer the question above, the Stanford Encyclopedia of Philosophy in the article, "Political Representation – key components of political representation," states four components exhibited by all forms of political representation. These are: some party that is representing (the representative, an organization, movement, state agency, etc.); some party that is being represented (the constituents, the clients, etc.); something that is being represented (opinions, perspectives, interests, discourses, etc.); and a setting within which the activity of representation is taking place (the political context).

To go by the categorization above, who is representing who means that there exist some party that is representing what could be a representative, an organization, a movement, or a state agency; and there could be another party that is representing constituents or clients.

Who is representing where and for what, according to Stanford Encyclopedia, relates to the setting within which the activity of representation is taking place or what it calls the political context. Representing for what, relates to something that is being represented, which could be the opinions, perspectives, interests and discourses of the party that is being represented.

In political or formalistic representation, the party that is representing and the one being represented could be individuals, constituents, groups, organizations or movements with the principle requirement that the representing party must have received the consent of the represented through some form of electoral process.

Humanity is directly responsible for all the underdevelopments hanging over its head. War is still being used as a means of resolving human differences and conflicts. Barbarism and extremism are still the order; selfishness and exclusion remain embedded in individuals.

Statecraft has improved systematically, metamorphosing from absolute monarchies through autocratic dictatorial republics, and now limping into participative democracy. Human beings learn at a reluctant speed; otherwise, no one can explain why since the 5th century tyranny and dictatorship triumphed for centuries.

Brutal regimes have raged across the planet terrorizing and denigrating human beings. At the initial stage of this barbaric leadership era, power rested in the hands of the war-making conquerors who ruled their human booty without any respect for human dignity.

As the warriors faded away, power shifted to the landowning aristocrats who used their feudal prerogatives to rule the commoners and destitute. Today power resides with the school-groomed aristocrats who believe that they were born to rule and as such ignore the downtrodden people in their management of public interest.

Whether it was in the era of the great warriors (who created bloody monarchies), or the feudalists (who manifested satanic greed), or the school-made aristocrats of today (who rule the masses with disrespect), representation has been completely absent in the warriors' era. It's been abused under feudal rule, and misinterpreted in the current scholastic born-to-rule era.

During the era of absolute rule, power was in the hands of one man who used cronies with satanic competences to reign over the population. The axe and the sword dictated the law; and the only way to live the next day was to submit to the dictates of the ruler who claimed to be owner of his people and their property; and therefore was at the same time representing everyone in whatever decision he took.

During the feudal era the landowning aristocrats used their affluence and influence to dominate and rule the masses, without any consideration to their opinion. The ruler treated with secondary landowners and major tenants, and had no serious business with the commoners. Privileged tenants constituted the middlemen between the ruler and the masses, and eventually met in some council to either inform or advise the ruler.

Such councils eventually developed to the king's council and were considered to be a form of de facto representation body. Selection of members to the king's council was the discretion of the ruler, and had no consideration of what the people were thinking; yet they made important decisions touching on the lives of those same people.

In the present era of the classroom made aristocrat, ruling the masses is rather more subtle and light-handed, unlike in the previous two eras. Governing has come a long way and the might is shifting in favor of the masses. The scholars who manage state power are enmeshed in the feeling that they were born to rule over the less- educated masses. They feel that they understand the craft of the state more than anyone else can, and therefore have the right to rule.

They are not as brutal as the previous rulers, but then they use such tactics to govern that can be considered in some cases as manipulative or deceptive. Here, they use parliament as a representative institution, but the question is: What type of parliament, rubber stamp or autonomous? The same ruling aristocrats write the constitution. This defines the nature of the state and the powers of parliament and the executive; and in this case, they will decide what body shall be more powerful.

In the present dispensation of parliament, the masses are still visibly not made present again because the distance between the represented and the representative is still practically wide. Who is representing who, where, remains a very serious question. Again, is parliament armed constitutionally to represent the masses? Are the men and women who sit in parliament representative of the masses? Are the masses conscious of the role of parliament and the relationship, which they are suppose to have with their representatives?

Even in the British parliamentary system, which is the mother of modern parliament, the questions above still do not find comfortable answers. Discontent is rife about the structure of representation, especially of the other regions in the Westminster government industry.

The discontent led to the historic independence referendum vote that was organized by the Scottish government in 2014 to decide whether Scotland should abandon its over 300 years union with Britain. Conflict between republicans who feel that they are not properly being represented in London, and unionists who think that it is better with London than alone, goes on and on in Northern Ireland.

Members of Parliament in Britain are hardly always in the good books of their constituents, as many do not see a direct link between what their representatives do in the Westminster Parliament and their individual and local expectations and interest. Parliament spends much of its time doing work for the government, rather than, putting the expectations and needs of their local constituents on the government table for prompt action and solution.

If deep misgivings still exist between the represented and the representative in an old parliamentary system like the one in London, then one can imagine what should obtain in the relatively new parliaments the young democracies of the world are groping with.

After experimenting with parliamentary representation in Britain for several centuries and not been able to obtain full satisfaction for the represented, new questions may be raised on the way parliament is conceived, designed and structured. Is the structure of parliament the problem? Or it is the people who sit in it who do not have a good mastery of how parliament should be run?

If the structure of parliament is the problem, then no matter how good representatives are, the problem of bad representation will remain. If the structure is good enough, then the problem becomes a lot easier to solve by simply selecting the representatives carefully.

It is important to examine the existing forms of representation, and exploring the advantages and limits of the concept of representation as a method of making present again a party that is physically or intellectually absent.

An interesting scientific classification and description of forms of representation is Hanna Pitkin's schematic analysis of the concept of political representation published in the Stanford Encyclopedia of Philosophy - *Political Representation, October 17, 2011, in* which, she distinguishes four forms of representation:

- *Formalistic representation described as the institutional arrangements that precede and initiate representation, and has two dimensions of authorization and accountability.*
- *Symbolic representation described as the way that a representative stands for the represented or the meaning that a representative has for those being represented.*
- *Descriptive representation described as the extent to which a representative resembles those being represented.*
- *Substantive representation described as the actions taken on the behalf of, in the interest of, as an agent of, and as a substitute of the represented.*

What are some of the advantages of representation as a solution to absenteeism? Before examining such advantages, it may be necessary to look at some of the qualities that a representative should have to be able to carry out his modest duty in political representation.

According to Edmund Burke in the, *Speech to the Electors at Bristol at the Conclusion of the Poll,* 1774,

"It ought to be the happiness and glory of a representative to live in the strictest union, the closest correspondence, and the most unreserved communication with his constituents. Their wishes ought to have great weight with him; their opinion, high respect; their business, unremitting attention. It is his duty to sacrifice his repose, his pleasures, his satisfactions, to theirs; and above all, ever, and in all cases, to prefer their interest to his own. But his unbiased opinion, his mature judgment, his enlightened conscience, he ought not to sacrifice to you, to any man, or to any set of men living."

James Madison favored representation, especially if the representatives possess outstanding qualities, when he said "this practice has several advantages, including the likelihood that the representatives would be superior to their constituencies in judgment, knowledge, and such skills as public speaking and negotiation."

First, the representative, present, helps the represented, absent in making decisions. The inability by everybody to be present during decision-making events makes representation indispensable. The absence of an interested party in a forum where decisions are made that will affect his life is always a cause for concern. The use of representatives is an attempt to solve the problem, whereby, though absent, a party can get another party, present, to make decisions on his behalf.

To backup this method, John Stuart in *Considerations on Representative Government (1862)*, states that "the only government which can fully satisfy all the exigencies of the social state is one in which the whole people participate ... But since all cannot, in a community exceeding a small town, participate personally in any but very minor portions of the public business, it follows that the ideal type of a perfect government must be representative."

Second, representation permits the represented to be absent. This is the central reason why representation came into existence; to manage the absence of the represented. Why is the represented absent? The answer to this question is as long and endless as the problems of humanity. Every day, the efforts and energy of man are focused on making life better; the coming of government to the scene is to help man to achieve the objective of good living. There is therefore a shared responsibility between government and the individual intended to help the individual and not the government to live a descent life.

The absence of the represented from decision-making circles is therefore not a deliberate exclusion, but an arranged stay away under the agreement that the individual could take time off from government business. Time off to concentrate on his personal life, while the government acting through his representative takes care of those problems that he is unable to tackle while acting alone.

Third, representation extends democratic participation and facilitates the process of decision-making. A single representative can receive the consent of a million or more people to represent them. This means that where ever the representative is acting, the million and more he is representing are considered to be acting together with him. The fewer the number of people participating in decision making, the faster the process is, because, the number of ideas to deliberate on are less and consensus is easier to obtain.

To buttress the fact above, Hans Von Rautenfeld, in *Political Representation: classical consent,* "the primary rational for the use of a system of representation was its usefulness for extending the reach of democracy over a community larger than could be governed through the direct participation of all."

Montesquieu commented that, "As in a free state, every man, considered to have a free soul, should be governed by himself, the people as a body should have legislative power; but as this is impossible in large states and is subject to many drawbacks in small ones, the people must have their representatives do all that they themselves cannot do". In line with Montesquieu, James Madison opined that, through representative institutions democracy can be extended over a much greater territory and population than had been thought possible until this time.

In the Federalist, November 10, 1787, Madison went on to stress the advantage of representative democracy, "Representative, as opposed to directly participatory, institutions provide more continuity and stability, as representative bodies are less likely than the people to act on sudden changes of opinion." He explained further that, "through the new science of electoral engineering a representative government can be made to aim more reliably at a general good that encompasses the interests and preferences of many, more reliably than if all individuals in the people were polled directly."

What is wrong about representation; is it practically possible to make present again something or somebody who is physically absent?

Representation entails two main activities carried out by the representative; speaking for, or doing for the represented. In exercising his duty, the representative can either speak for or on behalf of the represented, or he can either initiate action or be called upon to take action in the interest of the represented.

Linda Alcoff in *The Problem of Speaking for Others,* explains that, though elected representatives have a special kind of authorization to speak for their constituents, such authorization does not render null and void all attendant problems with speaking for others like, interpreting the other's situation and wishes. She goes further to reveal that the problem of speaking for others worsens when the speaker or representative does not belong to the same social group as the one spoken for or represented.

According to Alcoff, men cannot accurately speak for women, nor can white people speak for black people when she explains that, "The creation of women's studies and African-American studies departments was founded on the very belief: Both the study of and the advocacy for the oppressed must come to be done principally by the oppressed themselves; and that ... systematic divergences in social location (group) between speakers and those spoken for will have a significant effect on the content of what is said."

She discloses that, the practice of privileged persons speaking for or on behalf of less privileged persons has actually resulted in many cases in increasing or reinforcing the oppression of the group being spoken for.

These revelations raise serious concern over the present structure of the society, whereby anyone can claim to be talking for anyone. Women and men do not belong to the same social group, likewise children and adults; but in either case, the powerful group always imposes itself to be speaking for the weaker group. That is the general case where in the society, the powerful and privilege social group, men speak for the weak underprivileged group of women; and powerful adults speak for children, a vulnerable group.

To French philosopher Jean Jacque Rousseau, representatives are like mercenaries who fight in a war for a salary, but not for the objectives of the war. If representatives are truly like mercenaries, then their interests will have nothing in common with the interests of those they are representing, thereby rendering the process of representation risky. This view finds reason in two of four principles outlined by Bernard Manin to identify representative government in, *The Principles of Representative Government, 1997,* in which he reveals that: The decision-making of those who govern retains a degree of independence from the wishes of the electorate; and those who are governed may give expression to their opinions and political wishes without these being subject of control of those who govern. It's a conflict of interests here!

There is therefore ample similarity between Rousseau's qualification of representatives as mercenaries and Linda Alcoff's warning against persons from a privileged class speaking for persons belonging to an underprivileged class. When a rich person represents and speaks for a poor person, the tendency is for him to dramatize the situation of the poor, rather than feeling for him and protecting his interest.

Besides the human interest errors cited above, another important flaw of representation lies in the quality of the representative. Even in situations where the representative has been carefully selected and elected from the same social group as those he is representing, his ability to mobilize his full energy to push on with the interest of his constituents is always questionable.

Edmund Burke's speech to the electors in 1774 came to highlight the existence of the problem of the quality of the representative, even where the representative came from the same class background with the electors. James Madison, in support of representation, sighted as advantageous a situation where the representative has superior qualities in judgment, knowledge, and such skills as public speaking and negotiation, which the constituents may not have. The leaves us with the question: What happens if the representative does not possess such qualities as enumerated by Burke and Madison? The answer is: representation becomes a mess.

A lot of blame and skepticism has been placed on the representative alone, creating the impression that the represented is an upright and duty-conscious person. This is far from being realistic. The implicit agreement between the represented and the representative requires that both parties should live and work together in close collaboration and understanding. Practice has shown that this is not exactly the case.

The represented or the constituents are confronted by two weaknesses: complacency and personality conflict with the represented. Represented parties always fall victim to complacency in their relationship with the representative. In political representation, the represented in most cases interacts with his representative during the period of electioneering, after which all contacts between them is cut until the next vote.

This occasional contact between two parties who appear to share a common interest is surprising. It is easy to verify that the separation is caused by the represented, who seems to be more preoccupied with his so-called personal interest, viewing the activities of the representative to be farfetched and distant from his personal goals.

Generally, after an election, the voters disperse never to be seen together until the next election. They care very little about their representative or what he does during his term of office. Representatives who try to maintain regular contacts with their constituents are in most cases always disappointed by the irresponsiveness of their constituents. Absenteeism by the represented from meetings organized by the representative is always high as most constituents would prefer to take on their daily personal businesses than to go and confront their representative, thereby stifling accountability by the representative to the represented.

Complacency and indifference to politics and representation is an infectious disease that appears to have no effective cure in the constituents. The behavior goes on from the end of one election to the beginning of the next. Before the next elections, future representatives backed by their supporting institutions, go looking for the represented to beg, plead and woo the represented to get registered in the electoral registers.

During political campaigns, the representative and his agents for a second time will carry out an expensive and tedious march behind the represented to beg, plead and woo them to accept their ideology and vote for it. On the voting day, the worry is always about the turnout by the voters or represented. Afraid of low turnout and fear of losing the elections, representatives and the institutions backing them up do a last-minute flattering of the electorate to make them come out and participate in the voting.

The attitudes of the represented and representatives during an election period depict a businessman – client relationship. The one not interested in the product, and the other marketing the product to the other. Electioneering processes rather demonstrate two autonomous parties confronting each other, with one of them appearing to be active and powerful, while the other looks calm, observant, but not foolish. At the end of the tiring process of political campaign and voting, both parties retire to some rest; the represented go back to their daily personal interest business. The representative goes home for a short break to prepare himself for the complex role of middleman between the government and constituents, whose interests and ambitions are as diversified as the number of human needs for life.

Complacency is caused in most cases by the insertion of the middleman role of political parties, which have the technical duty to mobilize and educated the represented in politics. Unfortunately, political parties serve as a blockage to a direct contact between the represented and representative. Party loyalty has caused representatives to represent parties and not the represented, thereby making the adherence to a political party a prerequisite to having a representative.

Not belonging to a political party, or belonging to a party that has no representative, creates a feeling that one is not represented at all. The stress involved in militating and the infighting reminiscent of political party politics are frightening to many people, leading to the high numbers of complacent masses.

Personality conflict between the represented and the representative is the result of who the representative becomes once voted to the job. The authorization that is given by the represented to the representative to represent him is translated into representative power with special offices, creating a strong and powerful man, whose status becomes a no match to the individuals who gave him the power.

Scared by the new looks of their representative, the constituents are tempted to take a step or two behind to watch their agent from the crowd. Fear of the personality of the representative by the represented is therefore a serious issue in the relationship between the two parties; and its consequences on the system of representation are huge – mainly, the accountability right is lost by the represented to the profit of the representative who is saved the worries of questions and answers. Where tension caused by the conflict of personality between the represented and the representative is not diffused, and allowed to accumulate over a long time, the outburst can be explosive. Anger in members of a poorly managed constituency will lead to revolution, which could be peaceful or violent.

Lastly, the moral, logistics, legal and institutional ways and means that are given to the representative will greatly determine whether representation is a good thing or not. Edmund Burke and James Madison looked at the quality of the representative only, and did not project on the viability of the context of the representation.

How viable is the regime of representation in terms of the objectives and the means available to achieve such objectives? In political representation, do representatives enjoy the prerogatives required to carry out their duty effectively, or are representational institutions vested with powers required to accomplish their obligations? At municipal level, representatives will complain of restricted deliberative powers and overstretched coffers, while provincial and regional representatives will blame constitutional limitations to their ability to make certain decisions. And in the national parliament, representatives will complain about the domination of the executive with descriptions like rubber stamp, banana or kangaroo parliament rive.

Democratizing representation is the future of democracy that will take into consideration and try to fix the errors highlighted above. Making the representative and the institutions that he incarnates democratic will require an overhaul of the way human systems work. This will entail expanding the base of participation in politics and decision-making with consideration given to so call vulnerable social groups of the society – women and children in this case.

The inclusion of women and children in the political and decision-making processes is overdue; even though the process has been ongoing for a longtime, even if not formally. In our time, pressure is mounting on the society to review the way it does many things. Conservatism and old fashions are undergoing surgical criticism that is intended to create breathing space for some groups in the society. These groups have been victims for centuries of one form or another of neglect, suppression and abuse.

In the cases of women and children, a plethora of legislations and legal instruments are cropping up within national and international systems to define and implement the human rights of women and children. Among such rights awarded to these social groups is the right and freedom to live in the society, and participate in every aspect of its management. It is easy to verify that women and children do enjoy the freedom to live in the society, because indeed, they are here with us. The story will not be the same as concerns the freedom and right to participate in the management of the society. Again, it is easy to verify that women and children do not fully participate in the management of society, because indeed, they are hardly there with us.

The existence of new laws at the national and international level that seek to make present women and children in the heart of decision-making circles and events, signifies an excellent beginning for the march towards the genuine democratization of representation. The United Nations Charter and the Universal Declaration of Human Rights are both unequivocal on the equality of man, irrespective of sex and age.

Specialized legal instruments on the rights of women and children are easy to find prominent amongst are: the United Nations Conventions on the Elimination of All Forms of Discrimination against Women, and on the Rights of the Child. In Africa, the Protocol to the African Charter on Human and Peoples' Rights on the Rights of Women in Africa; and the African Charter on the Rights and Welfare of the Child. At national level, states are increasingly writing constitutions and passing laws that enhance the well-being and the participation of women and children in public life.

How democratic is representation, if we accept that democracy is a game of numbers determined by demography? It is no news that there are more women than men in our world. If representation were going to be democratic, then women would need more representatives than men. This is very serious because the nature of the state had changed long ago from being an industry dominated by power politics, to one dominated by the welfare of citizens.

If democracy is a game of numbers, and women have the numbers, then women should pull the shots in democratic representation. Women should especially represent women and speak for them in all social issues that are specific to women. It is outrageous that men continue to take decisions on issues related to the woman's social well-being. According to Linda Alcoff in the article *The Problem of Speaking for Others,* it is simply dangerous for someone from a different social group to speak for another person from a social group different from his.

Democratically, it is still to be explained why men who make up the minority do represent and speak for women who are in the majority. What is wrong here? If democracy is true, can one ascertain that political representation in the future will be in the hands of women whenever they might have decided to take things into their control? It is interesting to notice that women are gradually waking up from centuries of political slumber, and are systematically pushing themselves onto the playground of decision- making. More and more women go to school and through university. In many countries, females make up the majority of students in the universities, while more and more males dropout from school to pickup precarious, crude jobs like riding motorcycle taxis, working in garages, construction sites, etc.

Anyone who talks about welfare must talk about the diversified social environment of the society. With its new orientation as a social welfare state, governments have to come to terms with the fact that managing social issues are more complex than imposing public order. The complexity of social issues requires that targeted and expert oriented solutions must be sought. The social problems of women and children can never be the same as those for men. This means that whoever has to represent women or children, must master the social issues at stake and should be able to propose expert solutions to resolve them.

For the single reason that women know their problems better than men do, it should be forbidden for men to represent and speak for women in any formal institution of representation. Men should also refrain from making decisions in areas that are predominantly run by women, without getting the expert view of women. The same should apply to children's interest as well.

The coming on stage by several civil society inspired organizations and associations that promote and protect the rights and interests of women and children is a positive indicator for the future of democratizing representation. This is accomplished by bringing in women and children to become frontline players in political representation. Feminist NGOs and associations, as well as groups that specialize and focus only on the promotion and protection of women and children's interest, have been doing much in sensitizing and educating women, children and men.

CHAPTER 4

Democratizing Parliament

How democratic is parliament? This question is similar to the one that is asked by Robert Goldwin and William Schamber in the book *"How Democratic is the Constitution?"* relating to the American Constitution at the time it was fabricated. In the American case, the argument was between the Federalists who wanted a constitution that will protect corporate and elitist interests, against the anti-Federalists, who wanted a constitution that will protect the interests of the masses.

If a constitution is not democratic, any parliament created by it will not be democratic. Constitutional democracies are founded on a legal framework of law and politics where human liberties and freedoms are held at high esteem and protected. Democratic parliaments are therefore *constitutional parliaments* and not *institutional parliaments* in the sense that, the later is created and derives its powers and autonomy from a democratically enacted constitution; while the later is just another institution created or appointed by an agency such as the executive power, to serve a window dressing rule and make a system to appear democratic. *Constitutional parliaments* are found mostly in developed world democracies, while, *institutional parliaments* exist mostly in limping democracies found especially in Third World countries.

Early parliaments were institutions that were created by kings and rulers to serve initially as advisory bodies, and later as a forum for the masses to express their feelings to the rulers and governments. They were essentially undemocratic and had no real legislative powers.

The democratization of Parliament is a very long journey, which started several centuries ago. The history of the evolution of the British parliamentary system is the only existing consistent story that can be told about the democratization of parliament. A modern parliament emerged in England in the 13th century and was called the Curia Regis or the king's feudal council, which was comprised of: the king's tenants in chief, great barons and great prelates. The Curia Regis is what has become the House of Lords.

During the same period, the king started the convocation representatives of other lower social classes of the state like knights and burgesses, to acquire the consent of the masses to taxes levied by the king. At the beginning, the convocations were occasional, but repeated and eventually developed to become the House of Commons of today.

The 13th century was therefore the birth of the modern Parliament in Britain and the world. Since the two houses of Parliament came to existent, they have never ceased to exist; but have evolved from the kings appointed undemocratic *institutional parliament* to become a fully functioning democratic *constitutional parliament*.

Parliamentary sovereignty grew over the centuries through a confrontational collaboration and coexistence with the king. Sovereignty belonged to the king and the parliament was an institution that was needed to help the king in the exercise of sovereignty. As time evolved, the representatives in Parliament started questioning the legitimacy of the king as the custodian of sovereignty.

Persistent conflict over taxation and civil rights between the king and the barons who were also members of Parliament led to several standoffs, with Parliament emerging successful in several cases such as – the right to taxation ceased from being the king's prerogative to becoming parliaments; the increase implementation of the principles of the Magna Carta gave members of Parliament more powers and freedom to express themselves; the abolition of the monarchy by parliament demonstrated parliamentary sovereignty over the monarchy; the emergence of political parties within the House of Commons, set the ball rolling for a future democratic electoral system of representation.

Though Britain is the mother of modern parliamentary system, it does not mean that the best democratic ideas and intentions were found in Britain only; But the British experiment went on for a long time, without breaking up or being suspended or interrupted, as was the case in other states where the spirit of liberty and freedom from absolute monarchies were also clamored for by both the upper and lower social classes.

It should be noted, however, that the democratic revolution that was taking place in the British Isles inspired revolutions elsewhere in nearby Europe; the most prominent being the French Revolution, which happened only after the Britain had consolidated its inroads into democratic representation through Parliament. The French Revolution was the beginning of a long and tumultuous journey to democracy for the country, which today, is still classified as a second class democracy by some democratic expects.

It is true that, at the time the British people were battling to fix out things with their *"understandable kings,"* the people of continental Europe were suffocating under the heat of *"absolute power kings,"* with zero tolerance to any suspicion of disloyalty to their authority. Elsewhere, outside Europe, many sovereign primitive and barbaric monarchies existed; but they were eventually going to be threatened by the age of exploration, which eventually transformed into colonization.

Colonization became an important vector for the spread of democracy from Britain to the rest of the world. The present map of the democratic world gives a direct image of the degree of democratization that had taken place in the home country of the colonial masters concerned. The level of democratic practice in every former colony reflects directly on the level of democracy practice by the colonial master at back home.

Non-European countries that top the best democratic practices scale are predominantly former British colonies, most of which operate parliamentary democracies and fall under the developed world. This implies that democratic practice has instilled and promoted the spirit of development in these countries as compared to the vast underdevelopment that prevails in most countries that were not colonized by Britain.

Parliament is an institution that helps a country to create a national identity and sense of belonging. Through representative members of parliament, the people of the nation derive a sense of belonging to the fatherland. Parliament serves as a symbol of national unity and identity as every citizen can identify the representative from his constituency with those from other constituencies.

For the purpose of this book, democratic parliament will refer not only to the traditional national parliament, but also to the lower levels of democratic representation within a state at the local and regional or provincial levels.

Is the local council, local government or municipality democratic? There is a general tendency to limit democratic processes to transparent elections while, ignoring important factors such as: the quality of the participation by the population, and the representation of all the social groups in the institution elections are held for.

The quality of participation by the population relates to the group of eligible electors. What is the minimum voting age? Does a lower the age limit, mean higher voter participation for instance? The inclusion of all social groups in the selection of representatives to the local council is crucial to make it look democratic. Are women and children who constitute major social groups represented in the council?

Municipal or local government politics is crucial to the democratic life of a nation, for it is here that national politics takes root. Most politicians who animate national politics began their career in local politics; and the type of politics that practiced in the municipal scene will shape the quality of politics at the top.

Local politics has the necessary conditions that are required for beginners to take a first step into the game. It is important to recall that the system of participatory democracy that was experimented in ancient Greece in the 5th century was carried out at the village or community level. Because of its homogeneity and closeness, local politics is an excellent arena for women and children to begin practicing the art of participating in politics and leadership. The cost of participating in local politics costs far less such that, with physical efforts only, an activist can take part in all political events and contributions in kind may be valid at times. Because women are generally poor, local politics gives them an opportunity to get on board with little input requirement.

Considering that women generally make up the majority of the population of many communities, their exclusion from local politics automatically makes the process undemocratic as it is the minority, the men, who are often selected and elected to constitute the majority in the local council. If women become active in municipal politics, they shall as well learn and gain experience to participate at the regional and national levels.

Children are quite often described as future leaders; but then, they are often kept away from some events with no second thought given to the *leader of tomorrow* slogan. If we accept that a human being is never too old to learn, what makes us to think that a human being can be too young to learn? Children must be given full representation in local councils, especially in matters concerning the well-being of the child. Even if children do not sit in the council, they must be consulted and informed on any decisions that may be made to affect their lives, as well as putting in place a channel through which children's problems a tabled to the council for resolution.

For local councils or governments to be democratic, they must first of all be representative, that is, their structure and membership must take into consideration and reflect the social image of the society. If the membership component cannot resolve the problem entirely, then the structure of the institution of representation should provide official forums where matters concerning each social group can be tabled and examined. For example, chambers could be created to deal with matters touching on women and children's live in particular.

Regional, provincial or state government is the next level of political representation after the local government in many democratic systems. The appellations region, province and state stand for the same territorial unit or constituency; and in most cases are either headed by a governor, or a first minister. A region is made up of a several municipalities or local or local governments.

In most democratic systems, each municipality or local government elects representatives to sit in the regional council or provincial parliament or state legislation. How democratic is the state or provincial parliament? What is certain about most regional parliaments is that they have representatives who are coming from all the major communities of the region. This means that geopolitical representation is given priority over sociopolitical representation.

With representation based on geopolitical constituencies in most regional parliaments the institution cannot be seen to be democratic. The time has gone past when the constituency is limited to geographical space, and not to the quality and diversity of populations. Democratizing representation will require that constituencies be reshaped to enfranchise and give representation to social groups in a geographical area.

In some advanced democracies, representation has been extended to what is called disadvantaged minority communities or groups; but then, most of such groups can always be located to some geographical space within the national territory. Some have moved forward to introduce the quota system to increase the numbers of women in the various levels of parliament – local councils, regional assemblies and national parliaments. Good idea here, but then the women are not elected to represent women, but the entire constituency. This means that if she attempts to focus on feminist issues, she would be accused of sexism.

The issue here is representing the interest of women and children as separate social groups having special particularities, which the other social groups may not be able to understand or consider being worth deliberating on. Men can be as bad a representative for woman and children as it can be bad to recruit a seaman to pilot a spacecraft.

Democratizing regional parliaments will require that local councils be democratized in first place. As explained earlier, this can be done by restructuring the local government to provide special representation for women and child, which will give them the opportunity to officially present the problems that are special to their world; and by so doing, will engage decision-makers to look for solutions.

Regional councils will become democratic only after the local councils must have done so beforehand. It should be understood that representation at the regional level is more expensive and competitive; and it requires that any representatives must be trained or must have acquire some prior experience. If women and children must be part of any political adventure, existing barriers that have so far pushed them to back must be eliminated. Among the most limiting factors is the lack of financial resources.

Provincial and national politics are expensive ventures in which only the powerful and rich may want to venture, making it an elitist rather than a public business. It explains why traditional political representative institutions are systematically undemocratic, resulting in the conflict between the representative and the represented. The representative claims that he invested his personal financial resources to run the political processes, which led to his election; therefore, he/she is not directly responsible to the represented on whom he spent much money to get to.

Women and children do not have the type of money the powerful and the rich play around with to get elected as representatives. The rules of the game must be changed if these vulnerable social classes have to participate in the decision-making process of issues concerning their world. Contemporary politics is elitist at every level; it is even more selective and exclusive as we move up to the provincial and national levels.

Democratizing provincial parliaments will not mean increasing the number of women and children representatives, for these too risk becoming elitist women and children representatives and playing the usual elitist game. A more pragmatic way to democratize parliaments at each level is to create permanent chambers with institutional powers to meet and deliberate on problems specific to each group.

How democratic are national parliaments, generally known as upper and lower houses of parliament or national assemblies and senates? The general impression is that national parliaments are democratic, considering their geographical distribution of seats and constituencies. However, as seen earlier in this book, geopolitical representation alone, without any consideration given to social representation, cannot make a parliament democratic.

It means therefore that our celebrated national parliaments are NOT democratic and something has to be done to democratize it. The social representation component must be added to complete the process by bringing in our women and children, who by their very nature live in worlds different from the one perceived by men.

National parliaments are physically and strategically distant from the electors. What precisely is the role of parliament, some electors still do not comprehend. It is no doubt an elitist organization. Female representatives are always in minority numbers in parliaments and as seen earlier, they are expected to represent the entire people and not pay special attention to feminist problems in parliamentary work; otherwise, they are accused of sexism by their men colleague. Children are completely absent because they are accused of ignorance and innocence.

But imagine that, a chamber is put in place within the national parliament, to examine problems raised on or by women and children relating to special aspects of their lives?

The difference between creating special chambers in parliament for women and children is that creating chambers will provide an institutional forum, where the special problems touching on women and children's lives can be raised and examined at the level of government. While increasing the number of women representatives only, and giving children a seat in parliament within its present structure, it will not give either women or children the floor to table bills relating to their special problems. Creating women and children's chambers in parliament will make the institution more democratic than it is now, because whoever will sit in the chambers will have one task only to accomplish - speaking for women or children.

Parliament in its present style is overwhelmed by several lapses and weaknesses, due partly to its purpose and partly to its functioning. Such lapses and weaknesses are not hard to discern. As mentioned earlier on, the membership of parliament is essentially based on geographical constituencies and not on social constituencies. This area based allocation of representatives is out of phase with the diversity of social problems in the society. This means that constituencies ought to reflect the social stratification of the society and not land space in hectares or kilometers square.

Parliamentary procedures are heavily elitist and depend on experts to make things to happen. The process of law making is cumbersome and aristocratic, requiring more than one representative to initiate and pilot it to the end. This may explain why in the parliaments of most developing democracies, the initiation of bills to be tabled in parliament is predominantly done by the government. Parliamentarians are hardly seen to be initiating bills.

Unlike the two other arms of government, the executive and the judiciary, no one has ever bothered to explain why the legislature does not work on a day-to-day base. Law makers spend most of their time in recess. In Cameroon, for example, parliament meets only for 90 days in a year. MPs pass nine months together with their constituents and only three months for parliamentary work away from their constituency. Could we expect parliament to be active for the 12 months of the year, so as to make representation continuous and alive?

Periodic rather than continuous meeting by parliament makes the institution an absentee representative body, and as result, the amount of time that it puts in for real parliamentary work is very small. With little time available for real work, it is clear that the institution's performance cannot be the best. Private member's bills are nonexistent, and bills tabled by the government risk passing through without thorough scrutiny by the house. Parliament should learn to open its doors everyday like the executive and judiciary do.

One big deception that exists between the way parliament works, and the expectations of the constituents is that, while electors vote representatives to parliament and assign to them a local mandate to lobby to the government to carryout development projects in their respective constituencies, parliamentary work requires that representatives should have a mandate of national interest and not be limited to their constituents' mandate.

While the constituents claim that the MP from their constituency is representing them in parliament, the institution of parliament claims that each MP represents the entire nation, thereby, watering down

MPs' attachment and sense of responsibility and accountability to their constituents.

The dual mandate of representing both constituents and nation simultaneously, creates serious discomfort in MPs, who are conscious of the fact that; they have a responsibility to satisfy the expectations of their constituents who, have the power to change their representatives in the next election; but unfortunately, the way that parliament works does not permit them to realize the expectations of the electors. The principal activity of parliament is making laws whose origin is not from the electors; meanwhile, the main expectation of the electors is to see their local problems solved. As a result, MPs always find their job ridiculous and frustrating.

As representatives of both their constituents and nation at the same time in parliament the inevitable conflict of interest makes work difficult for MPs, reducing their diameter of work to endless compromises and consensus for the sake of the nation. Often, it is the interest of the constituents that is compromised for the bigger national interest. MPs therefore, end up serving the national interest while compromising the expectations of the electors in the process.

Executive domination of parliament is another challenge representatives have to deal with, even though; the level of such domination may vary from one system to the other. Despite its description as an independent arm of government, the role parliament plays and the way it operates makes many observers to belief that parliament is a child of the executive. This is easy to confirm considering the fact that, the government is often at the origin of the bills that are tabled for examination by parliament. As an independent arm of government, parliament is suppose to be the birth place of the law, and not a recipient of proposed laws, fashioned to the taste and interest of the executive arm.

Why do we need to include women, children and all social groups in the art of political representation? The answer is simply that all institutions of political representation must evolve and become democratic. In the physical sciences, evolution takes place on a permanent basis and new findings are developed, tested and used in improving the living conditions of humanity. In the science of politics and social art, excellent theories and principles do exist, which unfortunately are not being tested and used.

More than five centuries ago that the concept of geographical representation came into use, the practice has remain the same. But then, its ineffectiveness is visible in the general human underdevelopment and the extra suffering of vulnerable social groups like women and children.

The state and the government constitute the heartbeat of the society and define the destiny of the people. The people who manage the state determine what road the nation is going to take through the decisions they make. The type and quality of decisions that a state manager makes will depend on the type of training and experience that he has.

Because communities and nations are so big for any individual or group to be educated enough to manage alone, a plethora of institutions are put in place to facilitate the process. This means that managing a community or a nation is not the responsibility of a single person.

Because the state and government are the heartbeat of a nation; and because it is the people who run the government who decide the road its people are going to take, the purpose of this book therefore is to highlight the necessity to bring in women and children, in their right, into the management of the state and government. This will help to assure that the road the government will henceforth choose to take the people will not be hard for women and children to move on.

The plethora of government institutions serve as pathfinders and bulldozers that survey and fix the road path on which citizens move. Surveyors and drivers of the bulldozers are government managers, who in the present dispensation are dominated by men only, women and children being mostly absent. The presence of women and children in the survey and bulldozing phases will not mean sending the men home; rather, their presence will influence and guide the way the road is constructed, taking in to consideration that women and children will also move on the road.

Why should women be on board as of right in the management of the state? Again, because they are different from men and undergo special challenges, which men can barely imagine or completely ignore their existence. For example, men are aware that every woman experiences menstruation each month; but then, no man can imagine how the woman feels during such a period.

What does she need in terms of diet, medical and hygienic support to go through a safe menstruation? Who produces markets and distributes the napkins that she uses to control menstrual flow, at what price are they sold? Most importantly, are the menstrual napkins available everywhere and affordable to every woman and young girl? Let it not surprise anyone that men will be in charge of producing, marketing, pricing and distributing these napkins, where they give priority to profits and not service.

If women, wherever they may be living, have to undergo a safe menstruation each month, then they must be able to express the difficulties that they encounter during menstruation and be able to make proposals on how such difficulties can be removed. This will involve engaging consultations with all the actors who can contribute in removing the difficulties.

For any consultation with the sectors involved in helping women to go through safe menstruation, high-level representation will be required to give strength to such a negotiation. Through representation in government, women will be given the chance to influence and be informed about the production and distribution of such goods, which are essential and used exclusively by women.

The case of children is similar to that of women, but is more urgent. Unlike women who are experienced, strong, mature and resistant, children are ignorant, innocent, fragile, immature and vulnerable; meanwhile, the environment where they are growing is wild, dangerous and having no mercy.

The Soweto massacre of young people and children was just a tip of the iceberg, which forced the hands folded international community to institute the Day of the African Child on June 16, which some countries commemorate by convening the Children's Parliament – but it's not permanent though. Children have been and are still being treated like undesirable objects from conception in the womb to growing up in the cruel environment.

At the macro level, it is unimaginable and inadmissible that the law of war or the Geneva Conventions do not give a special touch on the protection of children. International Humanitarian Law depicts only two categories of people: combatants and noncombatants. This classification to my opinion is outdated just like representation based on geographical constituency.

The laws that guide the conduct of warfare and other hostile activities need to be revised and updated to give special protection to children. It is inadmissible for war commanders and ground forces to carryout military operations without any consideration as to how such an operation will impart the children who are living in the battleground.

Can you imagine the traumatized and battered faces of the children victims of the wars in Afghanistan, Sudan, Somalia, DRC, and most pathetically Syria? Humanity should be ashamed with these images of wounded, hungry, homeless, orphaned and crying babies, which cable television across the world brings into our homes.

At the micro level, criminal and evil acts orchestrated by adults against children are easy to come across. Mothers who eliminate children who are in the womb, starving children in many homes, battered kids here and there, abandoned babies and street children, child labor, child killing and kidnapping, non-education of children, school absenteeism and dropout, children psychological trauma and stress after divorce by parents, victims disease like HIV AIDS, contracted as a result of parents' negligence and carelessness, frontline victims of poverty and lack, and the list can go on and on.

CHAPTER 5

Lower House of Parliament

To insert chambers for women and children in the machine of parliament, will require a prior fingertips knowledge of how parliament works. How contemporary Parliament works is very vital for any proposed changes or reform to be well situated. It is therefore important to give a simple and straightforward description of how Parliament works. It will be crucial as well, to examine the importance of training political representatives, especially members of parliament who will animate any future democratized parliament, one that will see women and children speaking for themselves and advising policy on issues relating to their well-being. A new parliament wherein division of labor based on social constituencies rather than geopolitical constituencies will take center stage.

The lower house of parliament is one of the houses or chambers that make up a bicameral system of parliament. It is called lower house because there is an upper house with which it shares legislative power. This chapter will seek to explain how the lower house works.

Elected directly by the people, the lower house plays an instrumental role in the making of laws, controlling of administrative actions and public finances. It is more popular and dynamic in the animation of the legislative life of a country than the upper house. Members of the lower house are generally younger because the minimum age authorized to stand for elections to the lower house is always lower than for the upper house.

Lower houses of parliament are generally composed of members, who are representatives of grassroots constituencies distributed across the country. Constituencies may either be single member constituencies, where one candidate is selected to represent each constituency; or lists system constituencies, were a list carrying several members selected to represent each constituency.

Different countries have different appellation to their lower house of parliament. In some countries like Israel, for example, where only one house exist, all legislative function is fused in one. Where parliament has two chambers, each will have a name to identify and distinguish it from the other.

Titles that are commonly given to lower houses are: House of Assembly, Chamber of Representatives, National assembly, House of Commons, House of Representatives, etc. some countries use national or local names to identify their lower house, such as; Duma in Russia, Lok Sabha in India, Dail Eireann in Ireland and the Dewan Rakyat in Malaysia.

Lower houses generally, share certain features which make them look identical. For example their statuses have many elements in common such as: The direct election of members to the house from grassroots constituencies nationwide; the number of seats in the lower house is always more than that in the upper house, and is allocated proportionally with respect to the size of the population in each constituency.

Members to the lower house are always elected all at the same time in frequent elections, that take place at the end of each term of office for everyone, and the minimum age for candidates for election to the lower house is always lower. The role to authorize and control state finances and monetary laws are generally vested in the lower house of parliament.

In terms of the extra power wielded by the lower house, it can overthrow a government, especially in a parliamentary system through "a vote of no confidence" taken against the government. As concerns certain areas of legislation, the lower house may override or take precedence over the upper house. In parliamentary democracies, the head of government is appointed from the party with the majority seats in the lower house of parliament, and the government is answerable to it.

In most democracies, the impeachment and eventual trial of senior government officials like the president and ministers, and the decision to impeach, generally begins in the parliament specifically in the lower house; and the trial might be conducted by the upper house.

How is the lower house structured to carry out its day-to-day activities? Generally, the internal structure and functioning of the lower house is defined by a law made by the chamber called the "standing orders." Three major organs are: a central administration, committees and a plenary.

The central administration of the lower house is headed by the speaker or the president of the house who is assisted by a board or bureau. The principal role of the central administration is to carry out the day-to-day running of the house. Both the speaker and the board are elected by the house for a given term of office. In some systems, the term of office of the speaker and the board is annual, while for others, the term of office can be for the entire term of the legislature.

Besides the speaker and the board, there is a battery of technical and expert services and internal committees working at the background to implement the guide lines. These are put in place by the speaker and the board. These committees manage personnel financial and career requirements, procurement of needs and services, planning and organizing foreign travel by speaker and other board members, internal auditing of the house finances, etc.

Considering the fact that the lower house of parliament is a public institution, its internal management procedure will certainly be like for other public institutions, which is centered around, human resources, procurement of goods and services and internal auditing.

How the lower house is run internally has never been an issue of public interest; however, what the public is interested in, is the way the institution relates with it and the other governmental bodies, like; the executive, the upper house and the judiciary. The lower house relates to other institutions through committees of the house, which are defined and constituted in a professional way to make parliamentary work relevant and professional. Committees are defined and assigned specific duty tasks, which reflect the various sectors of government action, such as: the economy, social welfare, culture and politics.

Committees constitute the heartbeat of the lower house and the workshops of the house. Real parliamentary work is done in committees, which serve as "a vibrant link" between the lower house, the upper house, the executive and the public. Any reform of the lower house must target the committees. If women and children have to be awarded special parliamentary representation, this will take place through changing how committees are shaped and constructed.

The creation of committees is as a result of necessity and not obligatory. The Scottish Parliament, for example, is describes as a unicameral, committee-based legislature, so designed with the hope to make it more effective and powerful than the Parliament in England. Accordingly, Scotland adopted the committee system for purposes such as to:

- *Encourage significant public involvement in the Parliament's activities. To enable, individuals as well as members of organizations and groups to appear before committees or write to them to give evidence.*
- *Enable the Parliament to hold the Scottish Government to account effectively. This is done by scrutinising the work of the Government. Ministers do not sit on committees but can be asked to appear before the committee to answer questions.*
- *Encourage the sharing of power. Committees can investigate any item, which falls within their remit, hold inquiries and make recommendations to Parliament and the Government. Committees also have the power to initiate legislation themselves.*

In the Zimbabwean Parliament, portfolio committees are created to provide an avenue for citizens and civic organizations to contribute to the policy- making process through writing or why not attending committee meetings in public. Here, portfolio committees are fashioned in line with government ministries, to facilitate parliamentary understanding of how government departments work, and to be able to carry out the control of government action.

Using committees, the Zimbabwe Parliament has been able to enhance the governance system by bringing the executive to task in the way it draws up and implements public policy and programs. Through the system of working of committees, the participation of citizens in parliamentary affairs has risen to remarkable levels, thereby making the institution people friendly.

In South Africa, the role of committees in the lower house or National Assembly is to: Increase the amount of work that can be done by the house; ensure that issues brought to the attention of the house, are debated in more detail than in plenary; enhance participation by members of the house in parliamentary discussions; help MPs to develop expertise knowledge of committee's work; provide a forum for the public to present their views and opinions directly to parliamentarians; and provide an environment for parliament to hear evidence and collect information related to the work of a specific committee.

Committees in the South African National Assembly, have the following functions:

- monitor and oversee the work and budgets of national government departments and hold them accountable
- consider and amend bills and may initiate bills
- consider private members and provincial legislative proposals and special petitions
- consider international treaties and agreements
- examine specific areas of public life or matters of public interest
- take care of domestic parliamentary issues. *source: Public Education Office, Parliamentary Communication Services, Cape Town - www.parliament.gov.za*

Committees or *commissions parlementaires* constitute the workshops or laboratories of the lower house of parliament, be it in the US House of

Representatives, the British House of Commons or the French *Assemblee Nationale*. Membership of committees is always a small fraction of the entire house, and is selected in consideration of member's professional background and experiences. The largest committee of the house that can be created is the committee of the whole house, and constituting all the members of the house. With real work taking place in committees, plenary sessions are simply validation forums.

Plenary session is the big meeting of the whole house, organized occasionally during a parliamentary season, to validate and adopt or reject the report of committees. It obligatory that all the members of the house be present for plenary, which is normally chaired by the speaker. Representing the grandiose image of the house, plenary sessions are always highly publicized in the media and the validation procedure often takes place in public.

Public attention is often attracted more to plenary sessions than to committee meetings or central administration's work. As a forum where new laws see the light of day, the plenary is always of great significance and expectation to both the executive and the public. This means that after a plenary session, the probability is always high that new laws must have seen the light of day, to enrich the judicial and legal system.

As an institution, many lower houses enjoy the symbolic title role of representative of the people and the nation, and not representatives of constituencies. So because its members generally come from all the corners of the nation, and when they meet in the house, it is synonymous to the nation being united.

What is the personality of a member of the lower house of Parliament? The answer to this question can be as diversified as the background of the parliamentarians. An MP is in no way a small man or woman. Once their mandate is validated, they are showered with all sorts of advantages ranging from attractive financial packages, to immunity from random prosecution; in short, MPs are stars in their constituencies.

Legal requirements to become a candidate for parliament are general open and less restrictive. In general, stringent conditions like academic qualification or some form of professional experience are out of the way, creating room for everyone from anywhere in the land to try his or her luck in the parliamentary race.

A probable reason why academic or professional experience is not posed as condition to contest for parliament is a way to make representation in the house to be as diversified as the country itself. Men and women from different walks of life, who make it to parliament, constitute a mixture of people with different backgrounds, good enough to animate the various committees of the house.

The personality of a typical MP therefore does not tie to any specific academic qualifications, other than good behavior and some leadership skills manifested by the candidate towards the electorate.

No form of training exists to help MPs to acquire a uniform basis of reasoning and action. Even parliamentary procedures are not an issue for urgent learning by newly elected MPs. The absence of training for parliamentarians, explains why the role of parliament in all dimensions is not robust, in both space and time, and the domination of the executive is eminent because of the usually highly professional aptitude of civil servants, compared to little trained MPs.

Diverse backgrounds of MPs simply entails sluggishness in understanding themselves, delays in planning action, making parliament a reactive and not proactive institution. Because there is no common ground in thinking among MPs, the committee system was introduced to make up for the shortcoming.

According to experts, the importance of training MPs and politicians in general is always neglected; and both the press and the public do not seem to have the capacity for building MPs as crucial for them to effectively perform their functions. Imagine what the performance of a newly elected MP will be, if he or she does not receive induction lessons on parliamentary functions such as: the overall role of an MP; the skill of drafting bills and creating laws; Parliament's role in executive oversight; how the bicameral Parliament works.

The importance of training MPs, to build their skills to carry out parliamentary work need not to be emphasized. In the British House of Commons, the mother of parliaments, it was discovered that the institution was lagging behind other public institutions in training its members. This caused the chairman of the Committee on Standards in Public Life to emphasis that, the process to ensure that politicians are aware of their duties to be honest, open, accountable and selfless "cannot be left to chance."

Intimating that the induction process is the first training that new MPs receive when they take up their seats in Parliament, the chairman of the Committee on Standards disclosed that some MPs do not take the induction training seriously; and that, if the training is not compulsory, its programs including ethics should at least be "the norm rather than the exception" because, it is essential for public office holders to be aware of the standards expected of them.

To the Chairman of Standards, Parliament is at the apex of public life, legislating on standards for others in terms of regulatory regimes, holds to account those who fall below public expectations, and calls for standards to be imposed where it believes they are necessary. MPs must therefore be rigorously trained in ethics to enable them to preach by example.

In the South African parliamentary system, the need to educate members of parliament is equally urgent according to Hon Thandi Modise, Chairperson of the National Council of Provinces, South African Senate. In a speech to launch the training exercise for members of the fifth parliament, on June 3, 2014, he said that improving the skills of MPs, "Simply refers to induction, orientation and training through which new entrants to an organization acquire the necessary knowledge, skills, and behaviors to become effective organizational members and insiders. It is intended to allow participants to have exposure to critical information and knowledge pertaining to their work."

In the parliament of Canada one of the oldest in the world, the training of newly elected members is seen to be of great necessity. MPs are themselves conscious of the importance of learning new skills as the only way to improve on their performance in parliament.

According to a survey of the opinions of some Canadian MPs, carried out by Michael Macmillan and Alison Loat, one of the things that MPs needed urgently was training, "MPs don't receive much training. In fact, they're tossed into their jobs without any required background in economics, law, or public relations. The most training they receive is on what not to say, via the ample opportunities provided during elections to practice those do's and don'ts firsthand."

In the interview, Macmillan depicted a common worry among MPs, he said they, "Complained a lot about the lack of any kind of orientation, not knowing really how it works, being thrust into their job, without the *Party* giving them any real preparation. And that even though, they were front and center during their election, when they got to Ottawa, they became part of a larger machine where they weren't all that important. And that began when they had got no training."

The MPs complain discloses further that there is no process of evaluation, no regulation on how they do the job, and no training on how to do it. That MPs are abandoned the moment they are elected, only to be judged thereafter with fierce and fiery vengeance at every opportunity - be it the media or the next election. Macmillan concluded by asking, "Why not start with training MPs?"

Training members of the Pakistani Parliament is also an issue of prime concern, according to Sadia Saleem, "It is but natural to entrust our matters to people who are highly qualified and competent in their respective fields. The doctors who cure our illness, the engineers who build our houses, the lawyers who represent us in our law suits, and the managers who run our business, must all be professionally trained in their fields if they are to contribute positively in society and win our trust." In this line, he remarks that, it is amazing that we don't care about the education and training of the people to whom we hand over the pulse of our nation.

Saleem goes on to suggest that, it is important that the people to whom the rein of our country is entrusted should not only be equipped with the necessary educational capabilities, but be especially trained for this purpose. He said, "A training course should be set up where all the elected representatives are trained to execute their responsibilities in the correct manner, and are prepared to serve their country effectively and efficiently." He goes on to advise that, "On the basis of the educational and training program of the Civil Services, a program for the elected representatives should be chalked out."

Finally, he proposes that an academy should be established to offer training to MPs, based on a program that touches on all areas of politics, which might help them to effectively carry out their parliamentary responsibilities.

In Ecuador, parliamentarians received training on programs that focused on legislative and parliamentary communication, the functions of parliamentary media and the role of MPs in promoting transparency, accountability, citizen participation and contribution to building democracy.

Ken Coghill in Australia wishes to see parliamentarians acquire skills in parliamentary functions, which include: the basic functions of representation, legislating, and oversight, besides the traditional functions of deliberation, budget setting, making and breaking of government, and the redress of grievances. To Coghill, parliamentary functions must be discharged effectively and efficiently. For that to occur, parliamentarians supported by parliament's officials must have the capacities to contribute effectively to that discharge. He is therefore surprised that so little is said about these capabilities and how they can acquire it. And that's despite the fact that in other work domains, much is known about human resource development, for example, in business and in the public service, but very little concerning parliamentarians.

Advising on the necessity for capacity building for representatives, Coghill suggests capacity development for MPs based on programs such as: contextual understanding of the parliament's functions, deliberative and communications skills, information technology abilities, and ethical competence based on moral reasoning capacities.

Concluding his analysis, Ken Coghill raises this alarm "it has been demonstrated that there are widespread weaknesses in the development of the knowledge, skills and abilities that parliamentarians need in order to contribute to that effective functioning of the parliament. However, the unique features of each parliament dictate that parliamentary training programs must be localized and rigorously evaluated."

How democratic and accessible to all citizens is the race to the lower house of parliament? Are elections into this chamber within the reach of everyone, or simply an exclusive game reserved for the elite, the influential and the rich? Past and present experience has shown that the men and women who finally win seats in the Lower House belong to, or either rub shoulders with, such classes as elite, rich and the aristocracy.

This can be explained by the fact that, the processes to become an elected representative are intellectually demanding, financially expensive, and physically exhausting. Getting involved in the process entails an enormous and, at times, frightening sacrifices, which an individual working alone may not be able to support. Hence, the inevitable condition to belong to, or coalesce with the elite, the aristocracy, or the rich, in a cost and pressure-sharing union.

No explanation has been given so far as to why the process to becoming a representative requires huge sacrifices. But then, the consequences are severe on the quality of representation; instead of representatives being the direct choice of the masses, they are the choices of *ways and means*, which are not controlled by the masses.

The low numbers of women and the complete absence of children in Parliament is a direct consequence of the tedious road to be elected. No proof has ever been presented to show that women, who make up the majority of the population, are not interested in becoming parliamentarians or the people's representatives. Children are categorically pushed aside from the process, with no platform put in place to consult them on their interests. To Simone de Beauvoir, this is simply the outcome of man's dictatorship over women and children.

For example, men who make up the majority in Parliament may feel that they are serving children's interest by making a law that facilitates the importation of toys; good and fine, but then no one goes further to verify if the toys meet the expectations of kids and if at all they actually derive the same satisfaction from the toys as the adults who offer them expect. The truth is that adults force children to like anything to everything, even when other options may exists.

Once in Parliament, some MPs, especially newly elected members, come face-to- face with the realities of their new job. They step into the house with ambitions and dreams, which are not very different from those of their constituents; only to be taken aback by the limitations of parliamentary power and procedures.

Faced with the limits to their own power and influence to carve out things their way or the way their constituents are expecting, the spirit of the new MP begins to drop and he or she eventually devises a survival tactic consisting of manipulating the parliamentary system and their constituents, to be able to survive.

Few MPs can build the courage and honesty to explain to their constituents the very limits to their powers as members of parliament, and the powerlessness of the House of Parliament in defining and orientating policy so as to satisfy their constituents' interests and wishes. Members of parliament avoid such a disclosure wisely or foolishly for the psychological reason of fear of being undermined by their populations, who may see their representatives to be toothless dogs, and therefore of no use to them.

The central role of parliament as viewed by the government is to make laws, which are to be applied nationwide. But then, constituents in their various localities have a different view of what they expect to be the central role of their representative; that of an agent for development for the constituency. This means that, once parliament is elected, government confiscates the MPs from their constituents by deviating them from being agents of development for their localities, to law makers for the government. Constituents feel rightly or wrongly that they do not need a law for a school to be opened in their locality; they belief rather that they need a strong representative to negotiate and lobby for a school to be opened in their locality.

It is this discordance in the perception of the role of parliamentarians, between the population who elected them and the government who uses them, that representatives meet their waterloo in parliamentary life. Not long after taking up seat in parliament had the barrage of criticism started cropping up from the electors. The government, that controls the tools of development, does not give MPs the means to directly impact the development activities of their constituents as expected by the electorate who are waiting to see their representative to improve the local conditions of life.

Faced with the intransigence of government versus his ambition to satisfy his electorate, and the hungry expectations of the later, MPs gradually transform strategy and become absentees or promise dashing representatives to the grassroots. This behavior is always punished severely by the electorate who begin by calling their representative names such as liar, incompetent, manipulator, absentee representative, selfish, etc.

Before the next election, a good section of the electorate would have charged their MP for abuse of confidence, and classified him as incompetent and not deserving their vote come the next election. To prevent having embarrassed representatives, it is time the job of MPs to be scrutinized and defined in full detail, especially to the electorate so as to remove the imaginary conception that electors have about the role of their representatives in parliament.

Can the lower house of parliament be modified to accommodate women and children's chambers?

CHAPTER 6

Women's Chamber of Parliament

Political effort in the past centuries has been oriented towards the construction and fortification of the state, until such moments for example, when Rousseau projected the *Social Contract* and Karl Max the *Communist Manifesto*, that public opinion started to question the purpose of the state. Considering that the state has already traversed the stages of self-construction and consolidation, it is but imperative for it to be assigned a new objective.

The new objective of the mature state can be no other than the *welfare objective*. The well-being and survival of humanity should be the new objective of the nation state. To attain this objective, the vulnerable groups of women and children must be the focus of the new welfare state.

Welfare does not have a role in the land of the powerful and the affluence. Its place is in the country of the vulnerable and the poor. So there we are, in the present status quo of man's rule over women and children, the later automatically fall in the country of the vulnerable and poor. Women are vulnerable and poor, and are in need of welfare.

Different from men in several aspects, but not inferior or unequal to men in any way, it is important for society to reshape its views and interpretation of these differences. Sigmund Freud testified that he does not know who appointed man to lead women, while Gaston Bachelard suggested that it was the hammer and the anvil that enabled man to impose himself on women and nature.

From Freud's doubts to Bachelard's suggestion, about the myth of man's domination, reality has shown that women are simply different from men; but they are neither inferior nor weak as contemporary conspiracy theory depicts. What is positive so far is that, no one has yet contested the difference that exists between the two sexes. What is unfortunate is that many continue to consider the difference between men and women, to be a definition for strength and weakness. Men tend to represent strength and autonomy, and women represent weakness and dependence.

The principal difference between women and men is physical, and physiognomy tells it all, before dressing style and voice complement. From the face of a human being, it is easy to determine if the person is a male or a female, but for some rare cases where a female may carry the facial looks of a male and vice versa. Even in very young babies, the difference between the two sexes can be deciphered easily.

The face of the female looks smooth, soft, tender and less aggressive, and is generally ascribed the adjective beautiful; while the face of the male is generally less tender and more aggressive. Man is rarely related with the adjective beautiful, handsome it is said defines the good looks of a man. Feminine good looks are always showered with attractive description such as charming, angelic, sweet, etc. Masculine good looks are awarded heavy words like, good, handsome, gentle, humble, etc.

Besides the face, the structure of the body also provides a means to distinguish male from female. Grownup females carry a projecting chest below the shoulders filled by the mammalian gland or breast, and below the waist, the buttocks is far more muscular and protruding than in the male. The muscularity of the buttocks in either sex is to serve as a seat, the extra muscles in the female serves as a shock absorber during copulation.

The female body is generally softer compared to that of the male and no explanation has so far been given as to why this is so. If woman was created so soft to please man, what then is in man to please woman?

A woman's body is smooth, soft and tender, representing the fine conditions in life, but on the other hand, a man's body is rough and hard, representing the unpleasant state in life. Are women comfortable with the hard and rough touch of men?

Does a woman feel cheated by her man, when in return for her body smoothness and softness, man gives her his body roughness and hardness? Can it be an explanation for the theory of women enslavement to man? In what, therefore, does woman find pleasure in a man? Unfortunately, women are very secretive when it comes to talking about what they love in men. They quickly declare their love for their men, but will not give details. Younger women may disclose that they need men for their company and love; while mature and elderly women may intimate that they need men for protection.

Breaking the silence, some women have mustered the courage to speak out. Simone de Beauvoir in the *Second Sex* for example, comes out clear and explains that a woman needs a man for the penis he is carrying, which a woman does not have. According to her, a woman feel castrated by the absence of a penis, which she imagines had been slashed off from her and given to man.

From de Beauvoir's disclosure, one can suspect wrongly or rightly that a woman seeks to get married to man not out of the cause of love, but rather in a battle in which she intends to recapture a penis for herself. After all, the Holy Bible does not command woman to love her husband, rather, it exhorts her to submit to her husband. Through submission by woman to man probably, moral philosophers thought peace will reign in the marriage and will enable woman to secure her recaptured booty.

Convincing as it looks, when Beauvoir opines that women need men for the missing penis, men, according to most traditions and cultures, have always been accused for being the active womanizer and hunter of woman; little is known by many cultural setups about this hidden search for the penis being carried out by the secretive and reserved woman.

If women have lost their penises to men, it is easy to verify that men also, probably lost their breasts and buttocks to women. Can physiologists agree with me that the extra large breast that women carry were the mutilated testis, which climbed up to inflate the female mammalian gland? This is imaginable because the fluids that flow from the female breast and the male testis have both the same white pigment, and the one reinforces or completes the job that the other had started. Sperm from the testis penetrates and feeds the ovum, fertilizing it to become an embryo in the woman's womb. The baby that is born feeds on the milk flowing from the breast.

Another area of apparent, rather than clear cut difference, between men and women is in the way the brain works. Scientists have tried to find out how male and female brains work. Results from one such research revealed that male brains had more connections within hemispheres, whereas female brains were more connected between hemispheres, suggesting that male brains may be optimized for motor skills, and female brains may be optimized for combining analytical and intuitive thinking. According to Ragini Verma, an Associate Professor of Radiology at the University of Pennsylvania Medical School, "On average, men connect front to back (parts of the brain) more strongly than women, whereas women have stronger connections left to right."

Scientists explained that the back of the brain handles perception and the front of the brain handles action; the left hemisphere of the brain is the seat of logical thinking, while the right side of the brain begets intuitive thinking, suggesting that males may excel at motor skills, while women may be better at integrating analysis and intuitive thinking.

Medical experience has shown that when conception is not interrupted after fertilization the fetus is more likely to be female than male. This means than by biological preference, the creation of female is favored compared to male, and thereby resulting to demographic domination by the female. More women than men live in our world, constituting what political scientists define as the political majority. Numbers is always a big force in politics and economics and because women are more numerous than men, is demonstrative that they are different from men.

What has not yet been explained is why men, the minority, rule over women the majority even within a context tabbed democratic. Does the phenomenon find an answer in Master Wang's warning, which seems to suggest the triumph of physical power, intelligence and skill over demographic numbers, when he explains the difference between weakness and strength in Sun Tzu's Art of War? He warns, "When a cat is at the rat hole, 10,000 rats dare not come out; when a tiger guards the fjord, 10,000 deer cannot cross."

In the case of man and woman, can Master Wang's warning be the same as saying that man plays the cat and the tiger, while woman plays the rat and the deer? If so, does this lead to men's domination of women despite the number difference? Whatever the justification, cat or tiger, rat or deer, each one needs a space to survive. After all, the cat is at the rat hole not inside the hole, and the tiger guards the fjord and is not inside the fjord. If carrying a pregnancy, breastfeeding and having monthly menstruation is the role of the rat and deer, then taking the guard at the rat hole or the fjord to protect them is the role of cat and tiger. They are different roles that produce one result - continuity.

Women are quite different from men, but then, fortunately or unfortunately, they must share the same space. It is the sharing of this space that is causing the antagonism between the two sexes?

So far, all fields of progressive human social sciences have sought to either explain or make suggestions on how human beings can better share and coexist within the same living space. Philosophy, political science, religion, law, sociology, psychology and economics have all made useful suggestions to advice man on the importance and options available for a peaceful sharing of living space. Unfortunately, none of them has given a special touch to the special case of the woman who is generally represented by coded cultural jargons as just one component of the human system, thereby papering over her differentness.

What is the place of women in the sharing of the political, economic, and cultural spaces of society? Political space is that in which a society uses to solve problems of general interest, having to do with public service, taxation, law making and public security. Politics from the days of Socrates, Plato and Aristotle was the preserve of men in total exclusion of women and children. The situation has remained, and women are still mostly outside the circles of political space.

The absence of women in the political space renders not only representation incomplete, but the decision-making process defective. This is so because women's problems are problems of the society; and the absence of women in political space where problems are solved means that only half of the problems of the society are solved. Because women are different, they must be present to represent the difference. Men by virtue of their chemistry do not possess the audacity and functional capacity to deduce and solve issues that are specific and special to women.

Views of women and their interest on how public services should be organized and operated must be fully considered. This can happen only if women are present in the space where such decisions are made. For example, are our public spaces designed to accommodate the physiological difference of woman, office chairs and tables and toilets? Will a pregnant woman or one in her menses have access to hygienic cleaning facilities in the environment where she works or visits? The answer may be different in the developed and developing worlds.

Does anyone care to verify if the services offered by the public service take care of the specific and special problems of women? Working hours – should married women with children work for same hours, and leave work at the same time with men? Are women satisfied with the duration of maternal leave? Do they require home care and childbearing incentives? What consideration is given to woman the public servant, and woman the home manager? If men turn a blind eye to this dual management responsibility of women, should they be liable for the enslavement of women?

Taxation is an exhorting exercise concerning every group of society and women as a majority group are not exonerated from it. In the developing world, women are absent in the front line of corporate businesses, but then they sit on front benches in the small businesses of the background economy, which counts for the main force of the Third World economy. The vast majority of small and medium size businesses are owned and managed by women. How much consultation takes place to evaluate women's acceptance of the various taxes and the procedure to be used to collect such? Must women not be present at all the levels of the taxation process from, the creation of tax, amount payable, duration, procedure for collecting and penalties? Who elaborates the tax policy of the background economy, which is predominantly run by women?

Law making in the traditional and state setups is the preserve of men, from the village council, to the traditional clan council, the local council, regional assemblies, the national assemblies and the senates across the world, even in the canon and Sharia law circles men are not only present in sweeping numbers, but they pull the law making strings in all directions. In short, men make the laws with or without women around; no one cares, after all, the law is the law, and must be applied. Poulain de la Barre puts it this way, "Being men, those who have made and compiled the laws have favored their own sex, and jurists have elevated these laws into principles."

Poulain de la Barre had complained that men wrote the Bible, Koran, municipal and national laws; they defined the customs, culture and norms in the society. All of these were done when no woman was present and so, they made laws that favor the male sex. Men, are you guilty or not?

This accusation leveled on men is very serious and puts to question the very fabric of existing laws. Is it not time the entire law making machinery be reviewed and necessary adjustments made to take into consideration salient issues, such as democratizing representation in the law making chambers to include the issues of women by right?

Women are different, so must laws be made to take into full consideration this difference? How can a law to govern widowhood, inheritance, abortion, marriage, etc. be debated without the concerted and formal contribution from the women folk? Men working and deciding alone can never see the true face of the matter at issue, let alone decipher it. These acts and omissions should be criminalized or exempted.

Security is the protection of persons and property. Public security is government's effort to protect citizens and their property. What causes insecurity? The police and armed forces are instituted to guarantee security among humans. The power that is mustered by the security forces demonstrates that those who create insecurity are also as powerful. Which group of human beings is therefore responsible for insecurity in the society?

Women are described as weak and vulnerable, implying that they are in a constant state of danger and insecurity. Frail as a woman is, means that she can cause little harm to a man, but powerful as man is, it implies he can be harmful to the harmless woman. Men, not women, are therefore responsible for most acts of insecurity or threats to such.

What are the material components of insecurity? Are vulnerable groups consulted to get a full apprehension of what they feel about being insecure? To what extent is the insecurity that is lived by women taken into consideration, when secure men, not women, define operational security strategy for the forces?

Rape, street aggression, divorce, abortion, female genital mutilation, purse snatching, financial and material extortion, widowhood rights, inheritance rights, etc., constitute some forms of insecurities that are particular to women. Are men well informed and honest enough to define the full scope of these insecurities and guarantee women's optimum protection? In most male-dominated societies rape, for example, is not considered as a serious offence and many rapists walk free from the net of justice.

Divorce, although a legal process, creates insecurity to both parties; but then, if a woman is vulnerable, then the consequences of divorce turn to be heavier on her. In some male-dominated communities, women may find it impossible to initiate and push through a divorce case. Conversely, a woman may easily be divorced by her husband for a very trivial cause.

Widowhood is a new and unsecured title that women acquire when the most interesting stage in their live comes to an end, following the passing away of their sweet- heart husbands. No formal security measures exist to assist widows in the transition, all is left to chance. Lucky widows have a no worry testimony after the death of their husbands, while the unlucky ones testify the aftermath of their husbands with weeping eyes. International legal instruments make sweet declarations on the rights and privileges of widows, yet customary practices on the issue continue to take precedence over the faraway dreams of international law.

The plight of widows in India, for example, plenty in their numbers, is an eyesore for mankind. Humanity cannot continue to watch its women, who before the passing away of their husbands, had a home; but after their husband's death, are moving desperately from one camping condition to another in search of shelter and food.

Abortion is a serious threat to feminine security, both its causes and consequences. Women, who contemplate abortion, quite often find themselves in some form of insecurity, where abortion becomes an option for clearing the insecurity. Fear of bearing a child, without the accompanying support of a husband, creates a sense of insecurity in unmarried women whenever they become pregnant.

The legality or illegality of abortion is not an issue to be debated by moralists and law makers only, while ignoring the central actors involved in the act. The concerned actors and affected persons, young and elderly women, parents, pharmaceutical experts and medical professionals, must participate in the elaboration of laws on abortion.

Involving women in the abortion debate would result in the elaboration of a form of program for its prevention instead of a punishing law only. Why do women carry out abortions should be the first question to answer, before further measures are engaged to sanction the act. Contemporary antiabortion laws like most prohibiting legal instruments, is embedded in prohibiting declarations, representing legislative dictation. What is probable is that the laws on abortion focus on punishment, and not causes and prevention. This is typical of systems that are run by men, who will care little about the circumstances that cause a problem; yet they content themselves in prohibiting and sanctioning the problem.

It is a good thing to make a law to incriminate abortion because the lawmaker feels that, abortion is evil, satanic, murderous, and inhuman? But it is negligence on the part of the lawmaker whose intention is to correct the problem, to turn a blind eye to the conditions of the women who carry out the act? The aspect of prevention is absent in the anti-abortion legal process because the front line actors of abortion are not involved in the solution to the problem.

Inheritance and succession to family property continues to be a nightmare to females in many traditional communities, especially in the developing world. In such traditional arrangements, the woman is exempted from acquiring and owning real estate; land and housing, for trivial reasons; for example, that she would get married off and it would become the property of the husband's family. Or for the simple reason that a woman is herself a property and as a result, property cannot own property. Even in the United Kingdom, which is considered as the cradle of modern civilization, the discrimination of the female is still outstanding in the succession to the British throne, where a male child has preference over an elder sister to succeed to the throne. This means that had the parents of Queen Elizabeth II borne a male child after her, then Elizabeth II would never have become the British monarch.

This makes one to ask questions: Who made such laws? What considerations were given to those women who did not get married away, and to those who returned from broken marriages? What was the opinion of the women at the time t these rules were being put in place? Did anyone consult them? The homeless widows of India are clearly the victims of these manmade discriminating arrangements. Can the men turn around with a look of pity at our sisters, mothers and wives, who are living in destitution and abandonment across our world? To correct this stain on human dignity, women need to be given an institutional space to speak out and to be heard.

What space do women occupy in the grandiose economies of our nations? How do women survive in the capitalist dispensation of "survival of the fittest" considering the fact that they have been classified as the weaker and vulnerable sex? This is a serious case, especially if one has to come to terms with the contradicting facts that women make up the majority of our populations; they are weaker, but then, the economy is capitalist and requires that one must be "fit" and not "weak" to be able to survive in it.

Communism, which emerged as a possible correction to capitalism, produced far more flaws and proved to be more ineffective. The greatest weakness of communism was that it transformed men to women, and as a result, created more weak and vulnerable people than is desired by a society that wants to evolve and move forward. In the communist system, the only men in the society are the members of the politburo of the communist party. In this system, men are degraded to women, thereby, increasing instead of reducing the number of vulnerable people in the society. North Korea and Cuba are the only surviving communist states. And they are the worst places anyone may live in. Testimonies are there to verify this.

If men are the stronger sex, they are therefore the ones who are qualified and "fit" to survive in the capitalist economy. How do women, weak and therefore unfit, survive between the fangs of capitalist dragon? The response is simple: Women are the free riders, the beggars and dependents.

Trail young ladies when they step into their teens and observe how they begin to adjust and adapt themselves to hookup to the hidden survival economy of boyfriends. Young women are spontaneously induced into the marketplace of trafficking love for survival stipends. It is not uncommon therefore to find women carrying out full screening of the men who dare to seek for their hand in a love affair, to be assured that the new suitor would be able to pay the bills.

It is common for women of all age groups to share and fight over a man they consider to be financially viable and able to clear their economic basic needs. Love, which is morally considered to be a one man one woman affair, becomes accepted as a one strongman many girlfriends affair. Can someone say that the many girls enjoy sharing the one great man amongst themselves? Certainly NO! But what keeps them tight to the relationship is their ability to run their individual economies by tapping from the big financial guru. In fact, our young women survive on the boyfriend economy, which can be worth billions of dollars of love-provoked handouts offered by boyfriends to their girlfriends across the globe yearly.

"Survival of the fittest" the capitalist dictum is in full application here. In this scenario, a strong and fit male who successfully navigates through the capitalist ocean and makes a financial fortune for himself, will emerge before an audience made up mostly of the so-called "weak" and "unfit" women, who are preoccupied with how to get the next meal. Like in any other context of survival, norms are waved aside and preference given to the phenomenon of surviving today to be alive tomorrow. So the crowd of mostly young women would shower the man of substance with love sermons, and in return, will receive survival stipends for the day's bread. This is the manmade world according to de Beauvoir.

Older women, who must have lost their youthful feminine attractions, get retired to the backyard where they completely miss out on the playboys and their survival handouts. Even husbands turn to shift their loving eyes away from their one-time sweet- heart wives, onto more attractive and exciting young ladies. This has led to the generation conflict between young and older women, the former feeling that her own turn is ripe to have the men for herself, and the later is enmeshed in a fear of losing her man to what she describes as husband snatchers. Be it within or out of marriage, older women at this stage generally find themselves flushed out of the boyfriend economy and are abandoned to themselves.

Embarrassed by their new abrupt status, and with little or no academic or professional training, these unfortunate women (the majority of whom have already metamorphosed to become mothers and babysitters), begin to feel the bites of the fangs of the capitalist economy and its monstrous slogan "survival of the fittest."

Further weakened by age and the responsibility of childbearing and upbringing, and facing the harshness of capitalism, the abandoned women remain under the pressure to keep body and soul together. How do women survive under these high blood- provoking circumstances? Thanks be to nature that the human body was made with a capacity to resist the hardest of conditions and capable of undertaking the most laborious activities without falling apart.

From these conditions, the sweat economy has emerged. The biblical prediction that man will toil under the sun and the rain to eat, finds its full application in the sweat economy where nothing is left to chance. If you must live you must defy the odds by using body mechanical energy to make things happen before compensation can follow, usually in little crumbs.

How does the sweat economy operate? In rural communities in the developing world, take a stroll along a footpath leading to the farmlands on the hills and valleys in the sunrise hours, and you will observe the lines of women drifting out of the community in the direction of the farmlands. In the sunset hours the drift is from the farms towards the community.

The activity that takes place in the little farm holdings these women work in, is easy to speculate. Food crops and vegetables grow in the farms and the women will need them for a future meal and subsistence income, making it inevitable to take meticulous care of the crops. So these elderly women stoop down for several hours, using body mechanical energy to keep the crops protected and saved, to assure a good harvest. During the harvest, transportation of the produce from the farm to the community and eventually to the local market place is her duty. It is common at this time to see lines of these women with loads on their heads and backs, drifting from the farms to their homes and from their homes to the local village market.

Village markets show case the output of the sweat economy of the rural areas run predominantly by rural women, and serves as a link between the rural economy and the sweat economy of the urban centers.

In the urban areas of the developing economy, the women have to work as hard as their counterparts in the rural areas to make both ends meet. Abandoned to themselves, city women with little or no experience in commerce and trade, no access to takeoff capital, no market space to setup shop, etc., are often obliged to defy the odds and to kickstart micro businesses.

Millions of small businesses run by women across the world make up the sweat economy of the commercial centers in developing countries. Connected to their rural counterparts through the chain of markets, produce from the rural sweat economy finally end up in the sweat economy of urban areas, dominated by city women.

Even though city women carry out activities that look different from those of the rural women, they are also confronted by uphill and heartbreaking challenges. The exigencies of urban life make every aspect of survival difficult, and the micro businesses run by the women are always vulnerable in these harsh conditions.

Because they are very small, the businesses are located just everywhere and anywhere, at narrow roadsides in the suburbs and shanties, on the sides of city roads, besides public institutions, in unauthorized and non adapted spaces, and at the periphery or backyards of city markets. Small mobile restaurants are not uncommon as women in the food sector carry small pots and bulls full with ready-to-eat food on their heads, and move from house to house, street to street, bar to bar, etc., to feed the buyers and sellers of the sweat economy.

A large majority of the sweat economy in urban areas operates under precarious, unsecured, uninsured and unhygienic conditions. The city police are always seen chasing them and seizing their goods, which in most cases are exposed without any opportunity for shelter and lock and key. In some cases, the women and their goods share muddy, dusty, dirty and smelling market grounds, which expose them, and quite often the perishable food stuff they sell, to infectious diseases and contamination.

Besides the small business holdings, women get employed in short-term and low income jobs such as housemaid and babysitting in middle and upper class homes; young single mothers and school dropouts become servants in bars, restaurants and supermarkets.

Women and young girls, who cannot survive through these more conventional options of the sweat economy, take on a third option which is dubbed by some commentators as the oldest profession in history - prostitution. This is, in fact, a special type of small business operated by women across the world; and can be valued at billions of dollars annually. It is in short one of the cornerstones of the sweat economy and has such advantages as: noncapital demanding, no taxation, no license nor registration required, can take place anywhere anytime, etc.

In brief, this is how our women, the frail sex, try to survive in the harsh capitalist world that the men have instituted. And truly the men do not care an iota. From the boy friend economy to the sweat economy, the women eventually acquire experience, which over the years, raises them to almost the same operational capacity like the man. Widows succeed their late husbands as heads of the family and are able to keep the home together.

Because the lifespan of each woman in the boyfriend economy is on the average only a few years, the main base of survival for the woman is the sweating economy, which is effectively in their control. Considering the challenges that confront this very large, but vulnerable economic sector, I think the time is up for women to be given the voice and the platform on which they can influence government policy on issues that they understand and master better than men do.

In the world of culture and socials, women go in different directions from the men in several instances? For example, women dress differently from men; the two quite often belong to different cultural animation groups like dance and music, different sitting arrangements in some religious groups and traditional associations. In some indigenous setups, women and men have secret associations in which the other sex is completely exempted.

Women get distracted by activities that are different from those of men. It is difficult to know what activity distracts women most; it is also not known whether women would want to get the same forms of distraction like the men such as: watching and participating in sporting activities, or playing games and drinking beer in the bars. Women are often so secretive in matters of leisure. Maybe they lack the free time to waste in leisure, considering that she is always seen carrying out seemingly endless activities in and around the home. She is in short, in charge of a larger number of activities than men do.

Are traditional touristic sites designed in a way as to offer true leisure and pleasure to women whose true taste of leisure is not actually known? Tourism and leisure services experts will only get to know what women desire of their services, when women have been given the space to express and speak for themselves. I suspect that women hate or are simply indifferent to most of the man-imposed leisure activities, which they are always forced to visit and appreciate.

Women's chamber of parliament comes in here as an indispensable first step institutional initiative to start rewriting the story of woman.

Through this institutional representational framework, the world of the woman that runs parallel to that of man will be given its full identity and breathing space to survive. Without this official voice, women are suffocating under the armpits of men.

A legislative chamber for women's issues does not exclude men from participating. It will be the portfolio of the institution that will be exclusive for the examination of issues raised by women or arising from their daily activities. Representation in the women's chamber of parliament will be exclusively for women; however, men can be solicited for any expertise on some types of information.

Women, in the full independence of their chamber, will freely raise and debate any issue touching on the national, local and individual life of women, and come out with refined and implementable proposals. These proposals will then be tabled to the lower and upper houses of parliament for examination and eventual adoption.

The women's chamber of the house will have the function to assemble the problems affecting woman in the society, and to draft relevant bills that could solve such problems. The chamber will also serve as advisor to the government in the formulation of government policy on women. Hope is in the horizon for the eventual eradicating of the sufferings of women, because at all levels of the society, a lot of discussion and reflection is taking place. On the International Day for the Girl Child, 2014, UN Secretary General Ban Ki-moon presented the way forward to governments by making this appeal, "I call on all governments to take action to end all forms of violence against girls in all parts of the world. Together, we must create a world where violence against women and girls is never tolerated, and girls are always empowered to reach their full potential."

CHAPTER 7

Children's Chamber of Parliament

They are too many to be ignored, our children. They should not only be seen, but also heard. In Thailand, it is believed that, "Children are the future of the nation, if the children are intelligent, the country will be prosperous." In Tunisia, children are considered and treated as the future builders and developers of the country and the world

No child thinks that he or she is foolish or stupid because he or she is a child. Rather, the tendency is high for children to believe rightly or wrongly that they are more intelligent and smarter than adults. The only thing children regret not having is body height and size.

Children respect adults not for their age, but for fear of their huge body size. It is important that adults know this and stop seeing children as weak, foolish and vulnerable. I challenge adults to test children's capacity by giving them a chance to fully express themselves everywhere all the time. They would be surprised by the talent and good thinking they will demonstrate.

No ruler has been successful who does not seek to know the feelings and thinking of his people. Democratic governments rely on political free speech awarded to the public as a way to apprehend the ideas and views of the people, while dictatorial governments invest in spying and intelligence to capture public opinion.

The decline of dictatorships has played into the hands of democracy which itself, is under pressure to democratize. True democracy cannot be limited to the participation and acquisition of political rights by the male folk only, which has been the case for the past centuries that the terminology has animated politics.

Democracy like demography is a game of numbers and not gender and age. Children have always made up a large majority of the population, according to a study by the United Nations children's agency, the population of children in the world will increase to 90 percent of the next billion people. But then, children are permanently exempted from participation in politics and decision-making. They are told what to do, little or no room is given them to express themselves because adults feel that children have no experience that can enable them to make reasonable decisions.

Nowhere in politics is it stated that to participate or be consulted, actors must have excellent mastery of rocket science. The condition for participation in politics is unequivocal; all citizens must take part in the politics of their community. It is written nowhere that while the children hip-hop in the playground, adults in their armchairs, should take decisions on their behalf behind closed doors.

To complete the democratization process that was started in the 5th century, the large demographic number of children must be brought in to participate in the governance and development process of their community. This can be done because as stated earlier on, children are not as foolish and weak as adults may imagine.

After all, adults were children before; and they can testify with me that they were not as childish as not to know what they wanted for themselves and their community. As a child they can remember they always had a view or idea and, of course, a question to ask about everything taking place in the society. So why not begin now to tap from this large number of young visionaries who had been ignored in the past centuries, not for their ignorance, but because of ignorance?

By sidelining this large majority of children population from participating and contributing to their own well-being, and that of their community, the consequences over the centuries have been the neglect and suffering of children. It's described by an unidentified child activist this way, "Children are used as laborers in some countries, and immersed in armed conflict, living on the streets, suffering by differences, be it religion, minority issues, or disabilities. Children are displaced because of armed conflict, or suffer physical and psychological trauma. Soldiers are killing, maiming, abducting children, and attacking schools and hospitals. These soldiers are preventing humanitarian access to children. About 153 million children between the ages of 5 and 14 have been forced into child labor." This is just a tip of the iceberg of the suffering of children.

Children are small in their body size and consequently possess little physical, psychological, intellectual and moral strength to withstand the problems and challenges in life. Medical experts simply describe them as vulnerable generally. This entails that if children have to grow up to become successful adults, they MUST be followed up, assisted and protected by adults.

Absence of follow up of a child breeds immediate negative consequences on the child, such as neglect and exposure. The neglect of a child by his parents or guardians initially causes psychological trauma. This can manifest as a feeling of loneliness due to abandonment, and the feeling of not being loved by someone the child considers special to his life and well-being. Neglect can also produce an impression of premature freedom in a child when the feeling of control and restriction disappears from his surroundings. Neglect means abandoned to self, which can lead to idleness for a child who before was always assigned to perform duties within the home, but who eventually finds himself in a situation where no one no longer instructs him to do work. A child who enjoyed working at home, but who becomes idle, will face problems managing such idleness. They may seek a solution in child labor opportunities outside the home.

When follow up disappears in a child, he/she is automatically exposed in several ways: Uncontrolled playing, which often leads to accidents that cause body injuries and even loss of life; the new freedom to do anything and everything leads the child to abandon school and meet with bad friends from where he will eventually be put in contact with the great evils against the child in the society –becoming a street child, stealing, child prostitution, drug abuse, child labor, general exploitation, abduction and trafficking, recruitment to terrorist groups, and as child soldiers.

Absence of assistance to child is when a child no longer receives financial and material input and support from parents or guardians. This has a direct repercussion on the health and the upbringing or training of the child. If a child is deprived of assistance, his health is immediately affected by malnutrition, no medical attention from want of money to pay hospital consultations and medicines, no basic hygienic inputs, such as clean clothes and proper and regular bathing. All of these conditions will each contribute to destroy the health of the child, often exposing them to chronic and fatal diseases.

In the same line, when assistance is no longer given to a child, he/she automatically drops out from school or withdraws from any training that could help him to develop life-supporting skills needed to work in future and to earn a dignified living. As future parents bearing the responsibility to propagate and sustain the human species, it can be dangerous to the future of mankind that its future carriers will arrive on the stage bearing no skills to enable them to continue with the drama of life. No future for children, no future for the species.

Absence of protection for the child is a situation that goes beyond following up and assisting a child. Many children enjoy the benefits of both the follow up and assistance that they need, but it occurs quite often that they miss out on protection. Child protection is more or less a science that needs to be developed and promoted in the society.

Even within a good, complete home setup, children have always seen themselves undergoing uncomfortable situations, which human rights activist describe to be wrong and unhealthy for the well-being of the child. When the human rights or the rights of the child are not respected, he/she is exposed to severe suffering created by their own actions, and to abuses created by other people.

By not protecting children, they can be exposed to circumstances that they create by themselves, which will lead to suffering. For example, if a child is not well protected in his home, he would slip off home control to become a child living in the street. The regime of street children is a nightmare to any child who finds himself in the situation. The proportion of suffering such children undergo is satanic.

Where protection is absent, a child can easily slip over to drug abuse and prostitution. When the boy child if not protected, he can easily be attracted to smoking, drinking of alcohol and taking of drugs, which are all destructive to health; the girl child, on the other hand, if not protected, can easily slip into child prostitution, early pregnancy and marriage, which are all dangerous to the development of her still fragile body organs. The magnitude of suffering involve in child prostitution, early pregnancy and marriage are heartbreaking and frustrating.

Child abuse is often the result of the absence of protection. It is like saying that when you allow your doors open, dangerous snakes will creep into your home. A child who is not protected is one that has lost all his rights as a child and is exposed to human snakes who survive on children in forms such as: child exploitation through, child labor, low or no pay for the same work done by adults, child slavery through deprivation of rest and full sleep, recruitment into the army as a child soldier, and sexual abuse, victim of armed conflict, kidnapping and trafficking of children, victims of natural disasters and epidemics, etc.

Fortunately, much is already happening in the direction of protecting and emancipating children. The indicators are numerous and visible on the wall for all to see. For example, there are now days dedicated to celebrate the child; laws to protect the child; institutions and programs to assist and improve the lives of the child, etc., which are cropping up everyday everywhere across the world.

Symbolic days dedicated to the child have become a global phenomenon, with international and national dates chosen to celebrate and bring children to the fore. Before modern times, the Japanese as early as the 8th century started celebrating their children by dedicating separate dates to celebrate the boy and the girl child. Twice each year, Japan celebrates the child: the 3rd of March is devoted to the girls, and the 5th of May is dedicated to the boys.

Internationally, Children's Day was first proclaimed in 1925 following the World Conference for the Well-being of Children. It was not until 1954 that the United Nations General Assembly crowned the Children's Day effort, by proclaiming November 20 to be the Universal Children's Day; and encouraging all countries to institute a day to promote mutual exchange and understanding among children, and to initiate action to benefit and promote the welfare of the world's children.

Between these proclamations the Women's International Democratic Federation during its congress in Moscow November 22, 1949, proclaimed the International Day for Protection of Children, which was adopted by the countries of the former Communist Bloc in 1950 and celebrated every year on June 1, as Children's Day.

Following the Soweto massacre in South Africa in 1976, during which hundreds of people lost their lives when thousands of black students protested in the streets of Soweto to ask for quality education for black children, the Organization of African Unity or African Union in 1991 declared June 16 to be the Day of the African Child. This day is celebrated each year across the African continent. In Cameroon, it is commemorated by the holding of the Children's Parliament in the capital of Yaoundé.

Because of the specificity of problems encountered by the girls in society, the United Nations declared October 11 of each year to be the International Day of the Girl Child. The day is intended to give people and organizations the opportunity to raise public awareness of the different types of discrimination and abuse that many girls suffer from. It also gives the opportunity to promote girls' rights and highlight gender inequalities that remain between girls and boys.

Besides these international arrangements, the following nations have specific dates on which they celebrate Children's Day: Argentina, Armenia, Australia, Bangladesh, Bolivia, Burma, Brazil, Bulgaria, Canada, Congo, Congo DR, Cameroon, Equatorial Guinea, Gabon, Chad, Central African Republic, Chile, China, Ecuador, Czech Republic, Colombia, Cuba, Croatia, Costa Rica, Germany, Egypt, Finland, Russia, Armenia, Azerbaijan, Belarus, Estonia, Haiti, Georgia, Honduras, Ireland, Israel, Kazakhstan, Kyrgyzstan, Latvia, Lithuania, Trinidad and Tobago, Moldova, North Korea, Tajikistan, Turkmenistan, Hungary, Ukraine, Uzbekistan, Albania, Angola,

Benin, Bosnia, Bulgaria, Cambodia, Slovakia, Ethiopia, Kosovo, Laos, Malaysia, Republic of Macedonia, Mexico, Mongolia, Montenegro, Mozambique, Maldives, Nepal, Nigeria, New Zealand, Nicaragua, Panama, Peru, Paraguay, Uruguay, Poland, Romania, Serbia, Slovenia, Tanzania, India, Japan, Guatemala, Yemen, Indonesia, Vietnam, South Korea, Norway, Pakistan, Palestine Territory, Philippines, Portugal, Singapore, Sweden, South Africa, Sudan, Suriname, Sri Lanka, Spain, South Sudan, Taiwan, Thailand, Turkey, Tunisia, United States of America, Vanuatu, Zambia, Venezuela

Each country celebrates Children's Day in a different way, while some countries organize intense activities to commemorate the day, others are low key. The day is declared a public holiday in many countries, to allow parents to have some time together with their children. In Australia, for example, a national child care week is organized each year to take care not only of disabled, but of all children. In Bulgaria, motorists are expected to drive with their lights on all day to demonstrate vigilance over children on the highway. In Norway, Children's Day is celebrated alongside the Norwegian Constitution, to give children a special recognition.

In Thailand, the day is given the highest consideration in the land, with the King and the Prime Minister both relating with the children. Exceptionally on this day, children accompanied by their families, are allowed access to state structures through guided tours to; the Government House, where children visit the Prime Minister's office, the Royal Thai Air Force where children explore aircrafts, the Bangkok Bank where children are given school items such as pens, pencils and books. Children visit zoos and ride buses for free.

The institutionalization of Children's Day globally has come from a backdrop of a proliferation of laws and legal instruments at international and national levels which define and protect the rights of children.

On the international stage, there exists already a plethora of treaties relevant for the protection of the child:

- United Nations Declaration of Rights of the Child, 1958
- ILO Convention 138 on Minimum Age of Employment, 1973

- Hague Convention on International Child Abduction, 1980
- Convention on the Rights of the Child (CRC), 1989
- The African Charter on the Rights and Welfare of the Child, 1990
- Hague Convention on Inter Country Adoption, 1993
- Hague Convention on Parental Responsibility and Protection of Children, 1996
- ILO Convention 182 on Worst forms of Child Labor, 1999
- Optional Protocol on the Involvement of the Child in Armed Conflict, 2000
- Optional Protocol on the Sale of Children, Child Prostitution & Child Pornography, 2000
- Hague Convention on Child Support and other Forms of Family Maintenance, 2007

Besides this battery of international instruments to protect children, the rights of children like those of every human being are also defined in other important documents of legal force such as: The Universal Declaration of Human Rights, 1948, The African Charter on Human and People's Rights, and in the individual national constitutions of countries across the world.

Many countries have taken extra steps to design and implement interesting child development projects and programs. In Cameroon, for example, a Child Protection Code, and a draft Bill of the Person and Family Code documents are under elaboration by the government, which are intended to reinforce child protection and the rights of women when they become law.

Having being colonized by Britain and France, Cameroon adopted a *bi-jural* legal system made up of the English Common Law and the French Civil Law, a dichotomy that affects the way laws are applied in the English and French speaking zones of the country. To ensure that children enjoy the same rights and levels of protection in the two legal systems, an elaborate plan of action was published by The African Child Policy Forum titled Harmonization of Children's Laws in Cameroon.

The paper in what it terms *The Four General Principles* highlights interesting notions such as:

- **The best interest of the child:** Which can be depicted in several child protection instruments in Cameroonian laws and addressing such areas as; juvenile justice, social rehabilitation, matrimonial actions and labour relations.
- **non-discrimination:** intended to tackle such discriminations as, preference given to boy education and not considered a priority for the girl child, without emphasising the specificity of the problems faced by the girl child; and discrimination in the treatment of legitimate and illegitimate children, where the former enjoys full rights while the later is treated as an outsider.
- **The right to life, survival and development:** Which highlights the constitutional right to life and survival of the child, whether he is living with his biological family, an orphan or abandoned, or with physical disabilities?
- **Respect of the views of the child**: The institution of a Children's Parliament in Cameroon is intended to make children to participate in government management. Though its resolutions are not yet binding, they go a long way to influence government actions.

In this chapter, we shall be proposing that a permanent chamber for children's matters should be created in the national parliament of each country. In some countries, children's parliament already exists in one form or another, but play a symbolic rather than a legislative role. Some have been created and run by the state, while others are created by private associations.

Wherever a children's parliament in any form exists already, it should be saluted and encouraged as a positive step in the right direction. If someone somewhere already sees the need for children to have symbolic representation, another person will see the importance for real children's representation within the national parliament.

It is interesting to know that in political unstable countries like Yemen, Democratic Republic of Congo and the Central African Republic, children's parliaments have been established, not by the state, but by private initiative within an environment of full civil war and insecurity. Of course, children and women are known to suffer most from conflict and insecurity.

Necessity for a parliament for children is general; both the developed and developing countries need it, even though, the problems that children face may differ significantly in developed and developing countries, in failed states and in countries permanently in conflict; the need to protect children's interest remains crucial both in countries where UNICEF, for example, describes as the best countries for children to live, and those where the state does not even exist to provide basic protection for children.

In such countries as those described to be the best countries for children by UNICEF include: Netherlands, Sweden, Denmark, Finland, Spain, Switzerland, Norway, Italy, Ireland, Belgium, Germany, Canada, Greece, Poland, Czech Republic, France, Portugal, Austria, Hungary, United States, and United Kingdom, exclusively European and North American countries; the tendency may be to conclude that children are already well taken care of and a children's parliament may not be necessary.

The idea is that children's parliament are necessary to uphold and protect children's interest where they already exist (as in the countries above), and to create and protect such interest (where they do not exist), as in the countries outside Europe and North America, which are not included on UNICEF's list of best countries for children.

In the developing country of Yemen, a Children's Parliament was established in 2000 under the patronage of the non-governmental organization Democratic School with support from state some institutions like the Ministries of Education and Human Rights, and the Supreme Commission on Motherhood and Childhood. Its role is to, make children become aware of their rights and induce them to participate in decision making. It also has the duty to review and discuss reports about children's welfare in Yemen, and to make recommendations for handling problems that children face in the country.

The Children's Parliament was established in Yemen to raise issues about children and to influence the drafting of legislation related to children by giving the consent, feeling and the opinion of children for a better future for children.

The 75 members of the Yemeni Children's Parliament is made up of children between 10 and 18 years, who may not only be children of Yemeni origin. It is run but by civil society organizations, and not by the government. However, the government has ratified it and has provided accommodations for it meetings.

Commenting on the resolutions that they make Al-Mashari, a member of the Children's Parliament, explained that as a Children's Parliament they have come up with a set of final recommendations that convey the dreams of Yemen's children. And these recommendations will be presented to the government and the committee assigned to draft the new constitution, whose members will discuss them and include the ones that are appropriate in the Constitution of Yemen. Among the recommendations made to the government, he cited among others, demobilizing child soldiers, enrolling them in school, and providing food and medical help for them. One great victory that the Parliament has recorded is to sign a cooperation agreement with the Yemeni Ministry of Defense to reduce the number of child soldiers serving in the military.

In the Democratic Republic of Congo, a country in near permanent conflict, children in warring zones, especially in Eastern Congo, are abandoned to themselves and exposed to the lawlessness and impunity of war (hunger, kidnapping, rape, child soldier, forced labor and school dropout). In order to survive on their own, an organization known as Children's Parliament has been established, and it is run by children for children.

Created in 1999, the mission of the Children's Parliament in the DRC is to fight for the rights of children. Its members are elected by their peers from different districts, quarters and schools. All of them are young student parliamentarians who use their free time to carry out parliamentary work amidst huge obstacles and risks to their lives. They receive no pay.

To accomplish its mission of protecting the rights of Congolese children, Children's Parliament uses a double-edged approach dubbed child-to-child and child-for-child, whereby, in the former, each child is expected to directly help another child whose physical well-being is abused in the streets or anywhere. They do so by preventing or stopping any physical harm being meted out on another child. The later requires a child to be the advocate of another child where his or her rights are threatened or abused by using the child speaking for child approach, and soliciting assistance from elders or local officials.

According to Museke one of the young protagonist of the Children's Parliament in the DRC, they are passionate about their course and take pleasure helping and working for others. He says, "As long as there are people with problems, as long as I am alive, I will share what I know to help people change their behavior. You do not always have to wait to be helped. I think I have learned how to help others, rather than wait to be helped; and I want to share that knowledge."

What makes the Children's Parliament effort in the Democratic Republic of Congo unique is that it is not only an office-based institution, but is present in the streets organization as well. Parliamentarians take time off to seek real solutions for the day-to-day problems Congolese children face; they do so by either by alerting competent authorities in matters falling in their domain, or helping missing and abandoned children to rejoin their families. Besides, they are present in schools to educate children and students on their rights, and the need to protect and uphold such rights for themselves and their peers.

In the Central African Republic, where the state broke down completely (in 2013-2014), as a result of an interreligious conflict, a 32-member Children's Parliament now exists. It's a conflict that according to a member of the Children's Parliament in the Central African Republic, affected everyone, especially the children living in the interior of the country.

The role of Children's Parliament in the country is to protect the rights and interests of children in a war-torn environment, and to also serve as training ground for future leaders. To achieve its goal, the President of the Children's Parliament often meets government officials and United Nations representatives to inform them on the plight of children within the conflict. He uses interviews and debates on radio stations to sensitize and educate the public on children's rights and problems.

The Children's Parliament in the Central African Republic could just be the training place for future leaders in the country, according to the President of the organization, Christian Nzilkoue, "Being part of the Children's Parliament is preparing me for the future. It taught me how to work in a group and how to overcome difficulties." He told to Linda Tom of UNICEF through social media; he and his fellow parliamentarians follow the Children's Parliament in Cairo with great interest, and were impressed by the fact that some recommendations by the Children's Parliament in Egypt were presented at the National Assembly.

Because the state is fragile in this country, government support to the Children's Parliament is almost nonexistent, a situation that the President of the Parliament, Nzilkoue, views with regrets, "We need to get the government to take us seriously. In this context, of course, it is hard; we lack supplies and resources, but with just a bit of support we can do a lot. Every day, I can do something to defend children's rights."

In neighboring Cameroon, which is a relatively more peaceful country than Yemen, the Democratic Republic of Congo and the Central African Republic, another form of Children's Parliament exists. Two main differences between the Cameroon style and the three parliaments above are: First, in Cameroon, the Children's Parliament is fully created and run by the government; and second, it is a periodic institution.

Absence of conflict in Cameroon may be the reason why the Children's Parliament is not permanent as is the case in the warring countries, where children suffer most from the consequences of violence. The government of Cameroon instituted an annual Children's Parliament that holds a meeting every June, the Day of the African Child. This is done as partial fulfillment of conditions laid down in the

Convention on the Rights of the Child (CRC), and the African Charter on the Rights and Welfare of the Child (ACRWC), which require that member states develop at the national level, mechanisms for children's participation for the consideration of their views on issues concerning them.

Since 1998, and every June 16, a one-day session of Children's Parliament holds a meeting in the parliament building in Yaoundé, the capital of Cameroon. It is presided over by the Speaker of the National Assembly in person. According to the Ministry of Social Affairs of Cameroon, the organizers of the event, the main objective is to give children an appropriate framework to ensure the exercise of their rights to expression and participation. This is accomplished by promoting and popularizing the rights of the child, introducing children to democratic practices, teaching children the culture of effort, tolerance and respect for others. This influences kids to formulate and freely express their concerns, and to give their opinion on issues concerning them. This creates some consideration of relevant concerns of children in national policies and programs.

Children parliamentarians include 180 members in number, and they are elected by their peers from schools across the country. They each represent existing parliamentary constituencies of the Cameroon Parliament, such that for every Member of Parliament in the National Assembly, one child parliamentarian will be elected. The one-day parliamentary session is held in the presence of government ministers, who are invited to answer questions from children parliamentarians on issues relating to children's rights, welfare and education.

Being an exclusive government initiative, and considering that it is not a permanent body with nonpermanent members, the idea of Children's Parliament has to go beyond the Cameroon government's efforts to become a permanent institution.

In the developed world, the idea for a Children's Parliament was developed in Scotland by children who were attending a European environmental education project in Scotland. During their discussions in the forum, the children formulated a vision of an environmentally friendly city, where they created a Children's Parliament to be located in the city center. Their view being that children needed to be able to come together to talk about what mattered to them and that, "adults needed to understand that children's views are important and worth listening to" and that, "the word parliament means a place to talk and to listen."

Scotland has a Children's Parliament established on the premise to give children the opportunity to voice their ideas, thoughts and feelings, so that their concerns and opinions can be listened to and included in our social and political landscape. This is achieved by working directly with children through projects and consultations, and by educating and equipping adults with knowledge and skills to help them to replicate a Children's Parliament's strategies in their own locations.

A major objective of the Scottish Children's Parliament is to increase children's and adults' knowledge and understanding of children's human rights. The aim is of ensuring that the confident voices of children and the good listening skills of adults help to keep children healthy, happy and safe. "The wealth of experience and creative techniques Children's Parliament offers allows the child's voice to develop. Gaining a clearer understanding of children's ideas and thoughts is beneficial for life at home, at school, and in the wider world; and the Children's Parliament approach allows for more natural and honest reactions and feedback from children."

The children of Scotland seem to have understood and projected the course for Children's Parliament to interesting heights, considering the arguments that they put forward. Scottish children face problems that are certainly not the same as those faced by their counterparts in Yemen and the Central African Republic. But then, they think that their voice should be listened to by adults. The organization is one of the few who have the privilege of receiving support from the Scottish Government.

In Canada, as far back as in 1922, George Stewart started an initiative devoted to the development of leadership and awareness of the parliamentary system among young men and women of Manitoba. The initiative later developed to become the Youth Parliament of Manitoba, inspiring a network of similar organizations across Canada and the world; all of which operate on the same basic principle of fostering knowledge of the parliamentary system amongst Canadian youth.

In 1977, representatives from seven regional Youth Parliaments met and created the National Youth Parliament Association of Canada as a nonprofit organization. Members of the Association initially met biannually, and later annually, in the 1980s. It held its first meeting in August 1980, in the Senate chambers of the Canadian Parliament buildings in Ottawa.

The National Youth Parliament of Canada was created to serve the same purpose at the national level as the regional Youth Parliaments, which already existed in the regions, and had as motto: *"By Youth, For You."* And as philosophy: The firm believe that young people are entirely capable of running their own show; with a mission to: Foster amongst the youth an understanding of, an interest in, and an engagement with the Canadian democratic parliamentary process; and, in so doing, to encourage the growth of the individual and their abilities in public speaking, sharing experiences and ideas, as well as working together."

Unfortunately, the Youth Parliament of Canada did not live for long, due to financial difficulties in the late 1980s, when the association was unable to raise funds to sponsor its annual sessions. This, among other reasons, forced the Youth Parliament of Canada to go under by 1991.

CHAPTER 8

The Upper House

This chapter obtains exceptionally for bicameral parliamentary systems, and has no application in unicameral systems like in China, Israel, Albania, Armenia, Benin, Brunei, Comoros, etc. The relationship between the women's and children's chambers of parliament in unicameral systems will be as defined for the lower house of parliament.

The upper house is an institution that exists in a bicameral system of parliament. The application of modern bicameralism today has been inspired by the British parliamentary system, which is the oldest surviving parliament in contemporary history. The upper house of the British Parliament is known as the House of Lords and elsewhere it is generally known as the Senate, even though, some other countries have special appellations for their upper houses: *Bundesrat* in Germany; *Federal Council* in Russia; *Rajya Sabha* in India; *House of Councillors* in Japan, etc.

The House of Lords means a house where the lords or the noblemen in English society meet to give advice to the monarch and the government on matters of state interest. It started as an advisory council of powerful landlords and barons and developed into a lawmaking institution of Parliament.

The term senate was derived from the ancient Roman word *senex* meaning old man from, which came the term *senatus* Latin appellation for council of elders. There is no evidence, however, that the ancient

Roman Senate was an upper house of parliament that coexisted with a lower house at the time. It is easy to draw parallels between the ancient Roman Senate and the British *Magnum Concilium* or the *Great Council* that evolved to become the Parliament and eventually the House of Lords of the British Parliament.

Why do some countries use an upper house of parliament, when they could just say *"we are done with one chamber,"* like Israel? What importance is there to ride home about the bicameral system of parliament? What is the functional role of the upper house in a parliamentary system?

Why did the England develop a two-chamber system of parliament? During the reign of King Edward III, two chambers of parliament emerged from the existing Parliament with a House of Commons consisting of shire and borough representatives, and a House of Lords consisting of bishops, abbots and peers. The House of Lords emerged as the upper and most powerful chamber compared to the Commons, because of the quality of its representatives, who were the powerful landowners and barons of English society. The Commons was constituted of the downtrodden of society, and so could not whirl much political power.

With time, the power struggle between the two houses intensified and the outcome was in favor of the Commons, who saw its influence and power increased to the detriment of the lords. The domination by the Commons attained its apex at the end of the English Civil War in 1649, when the House of Commons through an Act of Parliament abolished the House of Lords and the monarchy. The closure of the Lords lasted 11 years before it was reinstated in 1660 to resume its role as the upper house of the English Parliament, a role it has exercised to the present day.

It should be noted that the origin of a bicameral system in England was motivated by a necessity for coherent discussion and debate in the chamber, and not to satisfy some federal or regional interest as was the case with most bicameral systems. The probability is high that class conflict between the influential barons and the downtrodden representatives of the shires and boroughs, made debates in the

Parliament uneven; and it was only but necessary to separate the two groups to meet separately where ideas and interests were identical.

The United States of America, the second longest surviving democracy in recent times, did not reinvent the bicameral wheel; it simply reshaped what it had learnt from its colonial master Britain. Coming out of a bloody independence war against British rule, the American Constitutional framers wanted to design a legislature that looked different from that in England. To do this, they decided to create an upper house that was based on ancient Roman parliamentary experience. Instead of a House of Lords as in England, they opted for the Roman option of the Senate.

Arguments between the federalists and the anti-federalists that animated the constitutional debates, and led to the creation of the Senate in the United States, projected two major matters at issue. First, the class conflict between the minority rich and majority poor; and second, the representation issues between small and big states. The main question was who should choose the people who will sit in the Senate? In England, the problem did not exist because, by the very nature of the House of Lords, its members were easily identified.

Constitutionalists, who supported the rich of American society, proposed a Senate that will protect the interests of the rich. This was to be done by restricting membership to the Senate to a few selected from the class of senior citizens with great achievements. The selection process was to take place through indirect and not general elections.

This view was strongly defended by James Madison, who warned that In England, at that time for example, if elections were open to all classes of people, the property of landed proprietors would be insecure. Because the Commons will take control of the upper house and pass an agrarian law to deprive landowners of their estate. And if he were correct, the U.S government ought to secure the permanent interests of the country against innovation. Landholders ought to have a share in the government, to support these invaluable interests, and to balance and check the other. They ought to be so constituted as to protect the minority of the opulent against the majority. The senate, therefore, ought to be this body; and to answer these purposes, the people ought to have permanency and stability.

Advocates for the majority poor argued that the Senate should be elected directly by the population, in the same way as members of the House of Representatives. Insisting that anything that is made to look a bit like the House of Lords in England will be undemocratic and against the aspirations of the American Constitution, which heralds the equality of all citizens.

Misgivings on the number of representatives each state sends to the Senate was raised by the less populated states who objected that the number of seats per state should not be based on the population of the state, for fear of domination by the highly populated states. These states already held good positions in the sharing of seats in the House of Representatives.

Compromise was reached, and it was decided that each state will have the same number of representatives in the Senate; and unlike the House of Representatives which represents the people, the Senate will represent but the states. Each state was to send two senators to the Senate, irrespective of the size of their population. The first Senate in the United States convened in 1789.

Canada had a similar experience to that of the United States in the construction of an upper house of parliament, in terms of the debates and the conditions that were at stake. Like the United States, Canada was a British colony with the influence of the Westminster parliamentary system dominating whatever options might have been available.

Amongst the conditions that necessitated the establishment of a senate in Canada, was the desire to unite the country. Before the Confederation of Canada was created in 1867, all British North American colonies, except British Columbia, had a bicameral parliamentary system. The Union between Upper and Lower Canada in 1840 set the unification train in Canada rolling.

In 1864, two conferences were held in Charlottetown and Quebec to discuss proposals for a union of British North American colonies, and so cropped up the debate on the role of an upper house of Parliament in the future federation of Canada. According to the Committees and Private Legislation Directorate, the Senate of Canada is a unique institution, being the single second chamber within the Canadian federation, and the only one in the Western world whose members are all appointed; and had there been no agreement to include the Senate as it is presently constituted, there would have been no Confederation in 1867.

To George Brown, a member of the Legislative Assembly and a framer of the Constitution, "The Senate of Canada was the key to federation - the very essence of our compact." He disclosed that, "Our Lower Canadian friends have agreed to give us representation by population in the Lower House, on the express condition that they would have equality in the Upper House. On no other condition could we have advanced a step."

Coming after the American Senate and the British House of Lords, Canadian constitutional writers had no reason to stress themselves in reinventing the wheel. In an article published in May 2001, the Committees and Private Legislation Directorate of the Parliament of Canada gives brief analysis on how the makers of the constitution were inspired by the British and American upper houses of parliament to create the Senate of Canada with its own specificities, however.

The Canadian Senate the article says resembles very much the British House of Lords in many of its parliamentary procedures, in its functions as a check on questionable legislation sent up from the House of Commons; and the fact that it is a non-elected House. However, the Senate differs from the Lords in that its membership is fixed, and that it is not subject to such constitutional provisions as the Parliament Acts of 1911 and 1949, which severely restrict the power of the Lords regarding the length of time it can delay legislation.

With the upper house of the United States the article explains that the Senate of Canada is similar to the United States Senate in its federal character, inasmuch as in both chambers the basis of representation is geographical equality. However, they differ because representation is based on regional equality as opposed to individual state or provincial equality, and because Canadian Senators are not elected and do not participate in ratifying executive decisions, the two chambers are quite dissimilar.

In France, a tumultuous long journey to experiment a bicameral parliamentary experiment started in 1795 when the "*Conseil des Anciens*" was created to serve as a second chamber. This was transformed in 1799 to "*le Sénat Conservateur*," which in its cession of April 2, 1814 proclaimed the overthrow of Napoleon I as leader of France. The period 1814-1830, known as the Restoration Era, saw the restoration of the monarchy and the experimentation of an upper house called "*Chambre des Pairs*," akin to the British House of Lords, a model which lasted till 1848.

During the authoritative rein of Napoleon III, an upper house similar to the previous *Sénat Conservateur* was instituted from 1851-1870. His rule was characterized by stringent press control, exiled opposition, and a weak parliament. The *Conseil des Anciens* and the *Sénat Conservateur* were not legislative bodies as such, but rather advisory organs on the model of ancient Roman Senate.

Constitutional reforms in 1875 saw the establishment of a republican senate in France *Le Sénat Republicain,* which lived till 1940, following the defeat of France by Germany during the Second World War. During this period, the French Parliament dominated a rather weak executive.

When France was liberated in 1946, the a new constitution was drawn, which reduced the powers of parliament and the senate lost its name of *Le Sénat* and was called *Conseil de la République*. It was until 1958 when the 5th Republic reinstated *Le Sénat* with all powers as an upper house of parliament. Back in full gear, the French Senate gradually consolidated its place in mainstream French politics, and since a last threat to its existence in 1969, the chamber has stayed on strong and working.

Between 1958 and 1961, France with the consent of its former colonies in Africa experimented what was called le *Sénat de la Communauté,* which was intended to replace the defunct French Union or *l'Union Française*. Newly independent Africa countries that wished to maintain close ties with their former colonial master France sent senators to represent them in the *Sénat de la Communauté,* which was chaired by the French President. The initiative was, however, short lived following the anti-colonial atmosphere that dominated world politics in 1960, the great year of African independence.

Germany unlike her French neighbor, did not experience a tumultuous ride to establish an upper house of parliament known as the *Bundesrat*. Founded in 1871 at the same time as the German Empire, the *Bundesrat* did not witness great turbulence nor undergo much transformation, but for a change of name from *Bundesrat* to *Reichstag* and a reduction of its powers during the Weimar Republic from 1919 to 1934.

Like most senates, the *Bundesrat* represents the *Länder* or the federal states, which make up the German Federal Republic. Members to the upper house are not elected, but appointed by the various *Länder or* state governments, most of whom are high level civil servants. What is interesting about the status of the *Bundesrat* is that the German Constitution does not expressly define it as the upper house of parliament vis-à-vis the *Bundestag* or the lower house, which is composed of representatives elected directly by the people.

The Federal Constitution of the Republic of Germany classes the President of the *Bundesrat* in the fourth place after the Federal President, the President of the *Bundestag,* and the Chancellor. The chamber is, however, very powerful in legislative matters and turns to be the heartbeat of the lawmaking process. It's very powerful position is drawing a lot of criticism from the other stake holders in the lawmaking industries, who are suggesting that the *Bundesrat* should be reformed to the American-like Senate.

It is possible to conclude with minimum error that most, if not all, the bicameral parliamentary systems that are operating in the world today learnt from or were inspired by the British bicameral system. Upper houses across the world share one or more elements in common with the British House of Lords. The senate found in many young democracies is either a photocopy of that of the former colonial master or an inspiration from the British or American upper house models.

What is the function of an upper house of parliament and what role shall the chamber reserved for wise people have in the new parliament of women and children's chambers?

Being the pioneer upper house in our age, the House of Lords in England exercises the function to scrutinize bills that have been approved by the lower house, the House of Commons. Except in some limited circumstances, the Lords may not prevent bills passing into law; it can delay bills and force the Commons to reconsider their decisions. By scrutinizing, the work of the House of Commons, the Lords acts as a check.

According to Encyclopedia Britannica, the most useful functions of the Lords is the revision of bills that the House of Commons has not formulated in sufficient detail' and the first hearing of noncontroversial bills that are then able, with a minimum of debate, to pass through the House of Commons. It is argued by some observers the Encyclopedia reveals, that, the House of Lords serves a valuable function by providing a national forum of debate free from the constraints of party discipline. Although the defeat of government legislation by the house has been relatively rare on major legislation, it sometimes does defy the government, especially the Labour Party governments. For example, 230 pieces of legislation proposed by the Labour government of 1974–79 were defeated by the House of Lords.

Before the Supreme Court was establishment in 2009, the House of Lords, through the Law Lords, acted as the Supreme Court in the British judicial system. Meanwhile, in the United Sates, the parliament still preserves the judicial role to impeachment top federal government officials. The House of Representatives indicts and the Senate conducts the trial.

The Senate of the United States, according to its founders, was created to serve as a stabilizer in the politics of the nation. Its founders had as intention to put in place an upper house that will perform amongst others, the role to protect the sovereignty of all the states in the union, big or small, by giving equal representation for each state in the Senate, two representatives for each state. The upper house was meant to represent the states, and the lower house to represent the American people like the House of Commons in England.

Another political stabilization role that the founders wanted the Senate to play was to establish a bicameral parliament, where one house will serve as a check on the other; thereby avoiding a possibility for a single house to become monstrously powerful. Thus, the Senate of the United States was established to serve as a check on the House of Representatives.

Like any other chamber of parliament, the legislative function of the Senate in the United Sates is obvious. For any bill to become law, the approval of the Senate and that of the House of Representatives is required. Working in synergy with the lower house, the Senate makes the laws that govern American society. Even though barred from initiating financial and appropriation bills, such bills initiated by the House or government, cannot become law without the Senate's approval.

Checks and balances is one value that is dear to American society and the Anglo-Saxon culture, where no institution or authority is allowed to hold absolute powers. The function of checks and balances performed by the Senate is put this way: "The Constitution provides several unique functions for the Senate that form its ability to 'check and balance' the powers of other elements of the Federal Government. These include the requirement that the Senate may advise and must consent to some of the president's government appointments; also, the Senate must consent to all treaties with foreign governments; it tries all impeachments, and it elects the vice president in the event no person gets a majority of the electoral votes." *(Source: unidentified)*

All appointees proposed by the President of the United States to top government offices and ambassadors designated abroad, must receive a pass from the Senate before they can pick up their posts. Treaties which the government initiates with foreign governments and international organizations also need the full approval of the Senate to become law in the United States. In exercising the function of Court of Impeachment, the Senate has tried two American Presidents: Andrew Johnson in 1868 and Bill Clinton in 1998.

The Senate of Canada has four principal roles according to a report by the Legal and Constitutional Affairs Committee in 1980: revising legislative role; investigative role; regional representative role; and protector of linguistic and minorities role.

Revising legislation is founded on the bicameral premise that one house has the responsibility to check on the other. The Senate of Canada is therefore called upon to revise or review proposed legislation that is initiated by the lower house, to ascertain its appropriateness with existing legal and societal norms. Besides this role, Senators also have the privilege to introduce private members' public bills.

Investigative actions by the Senate are carried out with the intention to clarify issues of public concern and interest. Through committees set up by the Senate and at times joint committees created by the Senate and the lower house, investigations can be carried out to either put light on controversial issues battering the life of the nation, or to help the House in making informed decisions.

Canada was created through a series of union agreements made with the different British colonies of North America, and like any negotiated union, the parties will always seek to put in place terms and conditions to guarantee their protection within the union. So, the Senate of Canada was created to represent the various regions and to guarantee their rights within the Federation. According to a May 2001 paper by the Committees and Private Legislation Directorate of Parliament, without an agreement to include the Senate as it is presently constituted, there would have been no Confederation of Canada in 1867; the Senate was the key to federation, and the very essence of the Canadian compact.

Protecting languages and minority groups was an indispensable prerogative for the stability of the union. Quebec condescended to the Crown on the condition that it would be spared it language – French. An eventual union between Quebec and the majority English-speaking regions of British North America necessitated a tacit guarantee for the protection of the French language in a unified Canada. The Senate was elected besides the Constitution to provide such a protection. Smaller regions like New Brunswick, Nova Scotia and Prince Edward Island all got representation in the Senate.

In France, the Senate or *Sénat* came a long way to instill itself in mainstream of French political life. With a tumultuous history, the institution was created like other upper houses to exercise a number of functions in the nation's public life, including: protecting the Constitution; making legislation; controlling government action; and representing the decentralized collectivities. The Senate in France also represents French citizens living abroad.

The German upper house *Bundesrat* performs a similar role as its counterparts across the world. Among others, it has three main functions: to represent and defend the interest of the federated states in relation with the Federation government and the European Union; it ensures that the political and administrative affairs of the federated states are incorporated in the federal legislation and administration and in European Union affairs; and it bears special responsibility for the Federal Republic of Germany.

Elsewhere in the world, in countries where an upper house of parliament exists, the role assigned to it will not be very different from those seen above. The rest of the world has simply copied what the older democracies have been experiment for centuries.

What are the qualities of a member of the upper house of Parliament? Membership to the British House of Lords is restricted to a selected category of personalities; Lords Spiritual and Lords Temporal. Lords Spiritual sit in the house by virtue of their ecclesiastical offices in the Anglican Church. Following years of reform, there exist only 26 Lords Spiritual in the House today, including: the Archbishop of Canterbury ; the Archbishop of York ; the Bishop of London; the Bishop of Durham; the Bishop of Winchester and the 21 longest-serving bishops from other dioceses in the Church of England.

Lords Temporal, who originally included several hundred hereditary peers and were ranked either as dukes, marquises, earls, viscounts, barons and Scottish Lords of Parliament. Hereditary peers are created by the Crown on the advice of the Prime Minister with the exception of members of the Royal Family. Before the dissolution of the monasteries,

Lords Spiritual made up the majority in the House of Lords; today, it is the Lords Temporal who have the numbers.

Qualification to be appointed to the Lords includes among others: The age factor, which requires that no person may sit in the House of Lords if under the age of 21. Nationality factor provides that only citizens of the United Kingdom can be members. Bankruptcy factor entails that any person in England and Wales may not sit in the House of Lords if he or she is the subject of a Bankruptcy Restrictions Order. Judicial record factor restricts and bars any person convicted of high treason from sitting in the House of Lords, until such person must have completed his or her full term of imprisonment. The gender factor was considered in 1958, and the first women were appointed to the House of Lords.

The qualification criteria for membership to the Senate of the United States, according to James Madison, required that members should possess a "greater extent of information and stability of character." According to the American Constitution, three main conditions must be met before an individual may qualify to sit in the Senate: he or she must be at least 30 years old; must have been a citizen of the United States for at least the past 9 years; and must be an inhabitant of the state he or she seeks to represent at the time of their election.

In Germany, qualification for appointment to the *Bundesrat* the Upper House of Parliament is restricted to high-ranking civil servants. In Canada, Professor Mackay describes the expected quality of those who are appointed to the upper house of parliament as mostly citizens who have already made their mark in life. Members are elected or appointed to the upper house of parliament are in short, expected to be wise men and women with full proof of experience and commonsense.

Within the new context of additional separate chambers for women and children, integrating the parliamentary system, the upper house of parliament will be expected to undergo some adjustments in it activities. The relationship and procedures of interaction between the new chambers and the upper house have to be established.

History has shown that, the relations between the upper and lower house of parliaments have been characterized more or less by conflict, the one seeking to dominate over the other. England started with a very powerful House of Lords as compared to a weak House of Commons; but today, the story is reversed, a Lords with much reduced powers and a Commons that make can make laws to cut the powers of the Lords to zero. Imagine a lawmaking organ that is barred from initiating acts relating to finance.

In the United States, the Senate maybe more powerful than the House of Representatives, with effective powers to check the actions of the later. However, the constitution bars it from initiating bills that touch on taxation, giving exclusive rights on taxation to the House of Representatives, which feels otherwise that the Senate does not also have powers to originate appropriation bills.

Conflict between the *Bundesrat* and the *Bundestag* in Germany is rife. Even though the *Bundestag* dominates the *Bundesrat* in legislative matters, the later plays a vital role in the legislative process, as it is required that all legislative initiative of the federal government must first be deposited before it in first place and then to the former. The *Bundesrat* has prominence over all legislation touching the interest of the federated states. The overriding power of the *Bundesrat* makes its critics to suggest that, replacing it with an American-style senate is going to moderate its blocking instincts.

Which house is going to block the legislation that will be initiated in the future women's and children's chambers of parliament? Will it be the upper or the lower house? The existing conflict between the lower and upper houses, if not carefully tailored, could be the first circumstance to frustrate their functioning.

The wisdom and personality of the members of the upper house will be required to create a favorable parliamentary environment for the young structures to pickup. The law should be able to protect the new organs of parliament from the crushing domination tendency of the old organs. The power of the upper lower houses to ignore or reject bills initiated by either the women's or children's chambers should be regulated in order to avoid contemptuous blocking and rejecting.

Using the experience and commonsense of its members, the upper house of parliament shall be called upon to babysit these new organs

which represent the most vulnerable social groups of the society. The senate, for example, should have a final say over bills initiate by the women's or children's chambers, which have been rejected or blocked by the lower house.

CHAPTER 9

Pain of Woman

What has happened to women? The problems that women face in life, is what happened to women. Problems faced by women have both natural and manmade origins, and are well documented in the modern society where freedom of expression and association has resulted in a scientific diagnosis of the problem, and with firebrand-type media coverage and public sensitization about them.

Women in developed and underdeveloped countries, women in rich and poor communities, educated and illiterate women, young and old women, all face problems which are identical in nature and caused by the fact that they are women. Plenty of scientific and expert publications have been made on the problems that women face in life; and the gravity of the problem is represented at the highest level by the creation of an agency for women known as United Nations Women. The causes of the pain of women can be classified in four categories: behavioral or intentional, natural, cultural, and circumstantial.

Behavioral or intentional causes of women's pain are those that emanate from the personal behavior and character of individuals. Male brutality or violence against women is a problem common to all levels and classes of the society. Domestic and love-related violence is reported by women in every society manifested in the form of regular or spontaneous beating of women and young girls by their husbands or boyfriends. In rural Pakistan, male brutality is carried out not only by husbands, but fathers and brothers are involved in brutalizing daughters and sisters. Extreme cases of male brutality have often led to outright death of the woman, or in permanent physical deformation in cases where acid or some dangerous weapon was used on the woman by the man. In Pakistan, extreme brutality against women and young girls resulting to dead is often described by its perpetrators as "honor killings." Young women have been murdered by their parents for as banal a reason as being seen talking to a boy.

In India, like elsewhere, male violence against women has been documented since the advent of records. Crimes include: rape, wife-battering, kidnapping and trafficking children as workers in brothels, dowry pressure on the woman, exploitation of young girls based on false promises of marriage, and job offers, etc. Rape and kidnapping rates in India are some of the highest, if not the highest in the world.

Inequality between males and females is an unannounced concept, which is not authorized anywhere; but which operates in all communities across the world. Nobody explains why it happens and few or no one dares to question why it is so. The ramifications of sex or gender inequality are numerous: Women are neglected in the day-to-day management of the society; they are never or barely consulted before important decisions are taken. Silent discrimination of the women is rife on the job side, in the pay women receive for equal work done, and in getting appointed to top positions and leadership role; women in short, are unrecognized. According to Samira Eshghi, the lack of confidence in Iranian women has created an almost unbearable glass ceiling for them, due to centuries of discrimination and humiliation, which has weakened their spirit and willingness to compete against men.

Sexual harassment is another recurrent pain woman and especially young girls have to deal with on a day-to-day basis. Young men consider and treat young women as sexual objects. Young men use slangs, commentaries, noises and physical touching, to intimidate young women. Men of money and power also harass women sexually, by making arrogant and denigrating sexual advances.

Roz Calvert in eHow presents sexual violence against women in Africa as follows: Women and girls in Africa experience the same kinds of violence and sexual violence that women in other parts of the world experience. A common weapon of war, in struggles such as those in Sudan and The Democratic Republic of Congo, is systematic rape. Women living in villages and refugee camps are targeted for rape.

With money and power, some men completely disregard the status of women even when they are effectively married and mothers. They feel that they have the authority to do what they want and get what they need from them. Sexual harassment is common in the workplace and is generally characterized by a boss throwing his weight on female subordinates in his service, or male collaborators taking advantage of proximity to forcefully obtain sexual relationships from female colleagues.

One blogger describes harassment of women in this way: harassment by men includes – continuous staring at women, making women the targets of lewd remarks, dirty jokes, repeated invitations to meals and outings, offers to drop them home, making unwanted comments about their dress, making "accidental" touches... and so on.

The ill-treatment of widows is not authorized in any society, but then individuals take it upon themselves to inflict pain and suffering on unfortunate women who have lost their life companions. It is not uncommon to see widows being accused of killing their late husbands and the punishment that always follows such accusations are severe; either the unfortunate widow is sent away from her matrimonial home, or she is completely dispossessed of whatever property her husband might have acquired. The deplorable situation of widows in India has attained shameful proportions. They are grouped in camps similar to those of refugees in war-torn countries, yet India is not at war.

Circumstantial causes of pain directed at women include those that cannot be associated to a specific actor or force, and are due to circumstances. Education, which is the main source of knowledge and power for every human being, is still an unavailable goal for millions of women across the world. Some individuals and communities are against female education by thinking that it is suicidal to educate women, who according to them are fit only for domestic duties. Even though the rate of education of girls has surpassed that of the boys in other communities, the nonexistent or very low rate of female education in those that object to it, signifies an installation of future long-term misery and subjugation of the women. So the circle of ignorance and not knowing what to do to change their lives will continue.

Women who work hard and attain positions of public responsibility become prisoners of their hard work; whereby, they are forced to accumulate the triple role of mother of the home, worker in her job side, and caregiver to vulnerable members in her home. According to one feminist, no one has yet reconciled how women and men are supposed to work and raise families, and look after the vulnerable especially when then women themselves fall sick and no one cares for them. Besides, she explains, if a woman takes time off to look after family, then she gets flack for not being fully committed to her job; but if a man takes time off to look after an ill parent, he is seen as a hero.

According to Michelle Bachelet, "When a man is dedicated to his job or politics, he is respected; but when a woman does the same thing and has kids, she's a bad mother." To her, obstacles conspire against women in the so-called economy of care that still expects women to look after the children, the elderly, the husband, the home; but women want to find a balance between work, love, and family.

The poverty of women is a circumstantial situation; no one can explain why the poverty levels among women remain highest in the society, even in communities where women enjoy maximum freedom and access to wealth creation facilities. In capitalist countries, very few women succeed to make it up to the club of richest people. Women in the grassroots of the community are swallowed in a near permanent grip of a frightening poverty.

In Africa, Vallely Paul describes the circumstantial pain of women this way; women work two-thirds of Africa's labor hours; they produce 70 percent of the food, but receive 10 percent of the income on the continent. Further, women own not even 1 percent of the property in Africa. The earnings of African women are spent on their children and households to a greater extent than those of men are spent on the same things. The challenges that face the women of Africa reduce their quality of life to a dangerous extent. Their life expectancy is 41 years.

Writing for eHow, Roz Calvert said, "All but two of the 30 poorest countries in the world are in Africa. Rural women are greatly affected by poverty. Men often travel to industrial areas to work, while women keep the rural economy running. They are subsistence farmers. Thirty three percent of people in Sub-Saharan Africa are malnourished. African women usually live without electricity, telephones or modern plumbing. When drought or floods ruin crops, women have no source of food aid."

Calvert describes other living conditions such as access to clean drinking water, HIV/AIDS and access to education by the African woman as pitiful. He explains that the lack of safe and clean drinking water is a problem for African women; more than 300 million people in Africa lack clean water. African women may walk up to five miles a day to fetch water. HIV/AIDS awareness organizations, Calvert explains, suggest that 59 percent of those living with HIV in Africa are female and pregnant. Women with HIV/AIDS lack access to drugs to prevent passing it to their infants. In education, two-thirds of the 40 million African children who do not attend school are girls. More than 53.2 percent of African women are illiterate.

Women empowerment initiatives have taken the courage to try to tackle the scourge of poverty women encounter. Such initiatives have focused on helping women to develop new skills in the creation and management of small businesses, and how to maximize income from traditional women activities like small holding agriculture, handicraft and service rendering. Women are equally educated on their human and economic rights and privileges.

The near absence of women in political houses and decision-making rooms, as well as from economic spheres, according to Michelle Bachelet former Chilean President and executive director of United Nations Women is a problem that no country has been spared from. The problem is quite circumstantial as many countries have widely opened the playing field to women, yet female participation has remained low. In cases where representational quotas have been imposed, women can be assured of a small portion of participation.

Describing the dismal participation by women in public affairs in New York Times, March 6, 2012 edition, Michelle Bachelet referred to countries in Latin America and explained that, "The biggest challenges everywhere are political participation and economic empowerment. No country is spared. Even in the most advanced countries, where women have been elected presidents or prime ministers, female candidates are still subjected to sexist jokes and comments, salary gaps persist, and there are too few women in major public and business positions."

Criticizing the strategy of allocating female quotas in business and politics, she said, "Electoral gender quota laws, however, do not seem to have smoothed the political path for women in Latin America, where at least 14 countries have quotas." And despite the fact that female presidents have emerged in their numbers in Latin America and elsewhere in recent times, she describes the upsurge as a paradox. "Female leaders or heads of state are not rare in Latin America. Today, women are presidents in three countries — Brazil, Argentina and Costa Rica — and 50 percent belong to political parties, but only 19 percent hold top positions." She concluded by saying that, "Quotas would find little favor in the United States, where women are only 16 percent of the 435 members of the House of Representatives and 17 percent among the 100 members of the Senate."

Culture and custom constitute one of the main sources of the pain women go through in the society. Forced and teenage marriage is a major problem in developing countries, and also a practiced perpetrated by some traditionalist expatriates who live in developed countries. Chronic poverty to a large extent and traditional practice to a lesser extent is the cause of forced and teenage marriages.

Poor families give out their young daughters for early marriage without seeking their consent. This is usually with the expectation that price paid for their daughter, and subsequent handouts by the son-in-law would improve the living conditions of the family. In some traditional communities parents choose husbands for their daughters, irrespective of whether the man's character is good or if the daughters like the man or not.

Commenting on the abuse by some cultures and customs of women's right to own property and the freedom of every woman to marry a man of her choice, Michelle Bachelet, Executive Director of UN Women said, "Women do not have citizen's rights; women do not have land's rights. Women should not be seen alone with a man in the street. You see women who have had acid thrown in their face because they didn't accept a marriage proposal or are killed because they didn't give birth to a boy. You see parents who give away a daughter for money or sex."

This practice has been the cause of many failed marriages, which often put the woman in a situation of uncertainty and misery. Forced marriage is perpetrated in some developed countries by foreign migrants, who insist on practicing their tradition even in countries where such practices are outlawed. In Pakistan, the horrible tradition known as *swara* sees women given away as a price to settle disputes.

The famous practice of female genital mutilation or (FGM), is one of the biggest evils that culture ever imposed on women. According to Roz Calvert, female genital mutilation, preformed ritually in some African cultures, is a violent and dangerous practice that women can seldom prevent. The slicing or chopping off of a young woman's clitoris with a knife or weapon is not only physically painful to the victim, but also psychologically barbaric and close to manslaughter. The consequences of FGM to the woman are: possible infection of the genitals, and lifelong sexual insensitivity. Cultures where FGM is practiced explain that it's a way to make women be faithful to their husbands.

Payment of dowry is been depicted as a source of pain to women especially in cultures where the ritual is strictly respected and applied. In many African cultures it is the man who pays a dowry fee to the family of his future wife. Here, the consequences of the ritual is not as severe on the woman, even though men have been accused for maltreating their wives with the claim that they spent a huge amount of money to pay her dowry. Men insult their wives by reminding them regularly that he is the one who paid dowry on her and not vice versa; so she has no voice and must only obey and remain silent.

In India, especially in Hindu culture, it is the family of the woman that pays dowry to the family of her future husband. The consequences of this practice are more severe on the woman, leading to serious frustration in the marital live of many women. According to Pranav Dua in "Essay on Problems of Women in Modern India," the practice is creating hell to women's lives in India; "The age-old practice of dowry has now assumed the form of a social evil because the bride's family is compelled to give some dowry as a price for marriage. It has become a social bane and a kind of bargain. It has caused unhappiness, misery and ruin of the bride's family. A huge amount of money is demanded at the time of marriage, and the failure to give the promised amount would make the bride to suffer the consequences at the hands of her in-laws and also the husband."

Pranav Dua explains that dowry is harassment where, women are ill-treated, disrespected, manhandled, tortured, and subjected to all sorts of cruelties. Newly married girls are the victims in most cases. In this situation, dowry is demanded as though it is a fundamental right of the bridegroom. In the case where the dowry is incomplete or is not paid at all, the woman will undergo – battering, neglect, abuse, starvation, hard labor and at times outright killing.

The practice of dowry Dua reiterates persists despite the existence of state laws banning it. Dowry related killings in India according to newspaper reports, were estimated at 4,148 in 1990, the figures increased to 4,366 in 1993 and 6,205 in 1994; that is a rate of one death for every 17 minutes. He feels that the practice leads to the degradation of women and reflects the inferior status of women in the society. "It makes a girl a great liability on her family's resources. Worst still, some unscrupulous and money-minded young men contract more than one marriage just for money. Some poor parents, who cannot pay a huge amount as dowry, are compelled to arrange the marriage of their daughters with old men, or physically or mentally handicapped persons and such marriages make the women miserable."

Natural causes of woman pain are depicted in: childbearing, child upbringing and family care. Childbearing is a funny and complicated period in a woman's life where her life and that of the embryo hang on the balance between life and death. Pregnancy is not only painful and risky, but also results in the transformation of the morphology of the woman. Expansion of the belly and the breasts and their eventual collapse when pregnancy comes to an end, with irreversible body changes body for of the woman.

Childbirth represents the peak of the risk involved in childbearing as medical statistics reveal. In every country, be it developed or developing, updated annual records exist on maternal and infant mortality rates, which give the number of mothers and children who die during childbirth. The figures are low in developed countries because of modern technology and improved medical practices, but are very high in developing countries because of the absence of these. Women therefore die in the course of trying to create new life. This is a factual risk that no man is exposed to. Men unfortunately are either unaware of the intensity of the risk their pregnant wives, daughters and fiancés are confronted with, or they simply ignore the risk and allow nature to take its course when the time comes. When the time comes, the painful cries of labor and delivery of the woman cannot be hidden, and the success of the process always depends on surrounding conditions of the quality of the midwife and existing support facilities for assisted delivery.

When the woman survives the child delivery process, the next big challenge she is confronted with is the upbringing of the toddler. She has to pay for bringing the child forth by feeding it with milk manufactured and stored in her breast, before future external feeding sources become applicable. Even when breast milk has to be supplemented, the responsibility is absolutely her own to collect and prepare the food and feed the baby. Daily care and handling involves regular cleaning and petting, premedical attention, vaccination follow-up, and the list goes on, are the exclusive tasks of the mother. In few privilege circumstances, babysitting assistance may be hired. Where babysitting assistance cannot be afforded, the mother is obliged to carry out her daily activities with toddler clinging to her body side.

In poor communities, it is common to spot working and toiling mothers with little babies tied against their backs or dangling on one lap, as the mother tries to accomplish one manual task or another. The innocent baby is forced to undergo whatever conditions that may encounter while hanging onto the mother; if the mother is performing an activity where her body vibrates or moves, the baby who is attached to her body will also vibrate or move at same frequency and speed as her mother's. If the mother is working under very cold or very hot temperatures, the baby must deal with the same temperatures; if the mother is selling in an environment that smells or harbor's toxic substances, the child must be exposed to the same, and so the adversities are endless.

Childbearing and upbringing is undoubtedly where the greatest pain of women begins, because these transform the body of the woman, imposes new constrains never realized before, and opens a new page of motherhood – owner and protector of another human being whose survival and future depends fully on her. That is how the good old days of girlhood and freedom fades away, relationships with men take a new dimension, and opportunities of playing around and getting things easy narrows down. Where the child is conceived outside of marriage, the embarrassment for the single mother is often great.

Young and inexperienced, she automatically finds herself overwhelmed by many responsibilities without the corresponding means to meet with the responsibilities in most cases. The baby is crying because it must eat, the child is sick and must be cured; her parents or guardians are all angry and disappointed about the unwanted baby she has brought to the family, yet they must take care of their daughter and her baby. The young mother is psychologically tormented each time she has to ask for assistance from her disappointed sponsors and philanthropists. What frustration these young mothers go through, nobody cares; that is how their morale is destroyed and their future put at stake. No one cares; they are easily castigated and classified as spoils of the community. The single mother abandoned to herself, is despised by the young men she could count on for marriage; child upbringing had forced her to discontinue school or whatever she was doing; she is locked out without income, but with a second mouth to feed and clothe.

When childbearing and upbringing takes place within the framework of marriage, the situation is a little bit more favorable to the woman in the sense that the father of her baby is there to support her in the child's upbringing; this is the case even though he did not share with her the biting pain of pregnancy and childbirth. Like in the single mother's case, child upbringing cuts down the woman's liberty and increases her responsibilities. Unlike the single mother, the married mother, besides her baby, has an entire household, especially her husband to take care of considering the norms of classical marriage. Traditional marriage assigns a *cahier-de- charge* or a duty of care that the woman must perform towards her husband. This implies increased responsibility even though assisted by the husband.

CHAPTER 10

Why Men Blame Women

Unlike complaints made by women against men, which are highly documented and published, complaints made by men against women are the least documented and published. One reason for this low profile open talk by men about women may be because of the tendency that men prefer to treat their relationships with women, and the problems that they encounter, with them as exclusive and personal.

Another reason could be that men think that if they make known the nasty experience and encounters they have with women, they will appear to be weak in the eyes of their male peers; since women are considered to be a weak sex and therefore should not manipulate man, the strong sex. In order words, a strongman should ignore rather than complain about what a weak person does to him.

In Cameroon, during weeklong activities leading to the celebration of the International Day of the Woman on March 8, the men always display plenty of restraint and quiet, as they observe with great vigilance and curiosity what women want to be up to this time again. They play the wait and see game, like a parent who allows the children to play while fully aware that he can stop the play at anytime necessary.

The men do not attempt to interrupt nor interfere with the Women's Day activities for fear of being brandished the bad chauvinists, yet they observe the occasion with all the attention and strictness, while waiting to see where things go wrong so as to pounce on the ladies.

However, in every community, it is always possible to stumble over some hot gossip on the frustrations that men have with women. In most discussions by men, relating to their appreciation of women's behavior, the impression is predominantly negative. Women are blamed and accused wrongly or rightly by men for almost everything.

Some common elements of character that men blame women for are: Women lie to and manipulate men; they are unrealistic and without understanding; they are extravagant, lazy, exploitative, money minded and selfish; women are disrespectful and cheat on their boyfriends, fiancés and husbands.

Women are generally accused by men for telling lies and manipulating in cases where the woman uses the man to attain her personal hidden objective. Young women often lie to men about their personality, level of education and their love status with the intention to impress the man; and in return get to be treated respectably, and to benefit with lucrative compensation and handouts from men. Many women lie to men about their marital status and relationship with other men, so as to encourage and keep them around to run double or multiple relationships. If the woman attains her objective through telling lies, her male victim is left devastated and feeling dubbed, manipulated and used by the woman. Where the man decides to revenge the woman's manipulation, the payback load in revenge is always alarming and explosive.

Young married women have the tendency to lie to their husbands, even when what is at stake is insignificant. This is usually caused by the spillover effect of the old celibacy habit of lying and manipulating men; after all, her husband is just another man that she recruited from the lot that clamored for her charm and beauty. Why should he be treated specially?

Women are unrealistic and without understanding is a character that is predominant in young women, whose men accuse them of living in a dreamland, composed of disproportionate wishes and elusive expectations. Every young woman grows up with the feeling and dream that she must get married to the richest, most handsome and most intelligent man in the society. At an early age, they try to enforce this dream, by meticulously selecting the men they date, so as to reduce to minimum any errors that may thwart the dream.

When the pressure of nature begins to mount, young women in the form of time, age, and obligation to survive, adopt tricks and manipulation to get the best men for themselves as guarantee to a better life. Considering that there are always just a few good men for so many women, the majority are always forced to accept those men they had initially despised as downtrodden and not up to standards.

This is where trouble begins, because the young woman accepts the man as her partner, but refuses to accept his substandard status. She had actually despised before and she will not accept it until much later in life. Fully aware that her new choice of partner is not up to what she initially dreamed to have, the woman dishonestly refuses to cut down her dream to her new man's size; but insists on attaining the big dream with a lesser man. This approach is nothing different from unrealism, which is the cause of not understanding, which men accuse women of. In principle, women accept men but refuse their status.

Women are extravagant, lazy, exploitative, money minded and selfish – this is the a,b,c definition of women by men. Women until later in their lives try to take advantage of the sex discrimination of society and want to retreat to the dependency status of free riders, while men do the hard labor on their behalf. As free riders of fortune, young women expect men to provide for all their needs in life, while they make no effort to help themselves.

Though dependent on the men, women's taste for luxury is always frightening to their male sponsors, who toil to make the big income. Their desire for money is alarming, yet no one holds them accountable for the expenditures that they make, since money is given to them for free and they spend it freely. Men consider the frequent request for money that women make to them as irrational, dubious and unfounded. It is not uncommon to hear men complaining that they do not know what their women do with their money. They explain that when a man urgently needs money their female partners are always indifferent, while some refuse deliberately to help their men even when they have money ready in their purse.

One more complaint from men against women is that they are disrespectful and cheat on their boyfriends, fiancés and husbands. Because the majority of women get married to men who were not their initial choice or dream husband, the tendency is for her to underrate and undermine him most of the time.

Where the woman thinks that her man is not the strongman she had dreamt to have, she gets furious and irritated, causing her to manifest periodic comportments of frustration and regret for her choice. Because she cannot walk away easily from the relationship because of the constraints of marriage, she seeks refuge in such behaviors as – disrespect and stubbornness and in serious situations, the woman cheats on her husband with impunity.

In the precarious regimes of fiancé and boyfriend, women feel that they still enjoy the full liberty to play around with their love life. Difficult it is therefore to come across young women who are faithful to fiancés, not to talk of to boyfriends. Every man is enmeshed in the suspicion of his wife, fiancé or girlfriend; they are frivolous and wild in their desire to capture new men blessed of substance and affluence.

Women feel that their husbands and boyfriends do not meet their expectation; they are not their dream men, and consequently do not satisfy their vision. So women go out to the wild hunting and fishing for the unknown dream man of their vision, and that's how infidelity and unfaithfulness are amplified. Just take a look on how women and young girls are using the internet today, and what you will find out is just enough for you to erase the words fidelity and faithfulness in man/ woman relationships.

The coming of cell phones and the internet has given an opportunity to society to understand the true chemistry of the woman and her feminine egos. Cell phones have facilitated the process for recruiting new partners, and women take great advantage of this. It is not uncommon for a woman who is accompanied by her husband or boyfriend to slip her telephone number to another man standing or sitting close to her in a gathering or public place. With the telephone, courtship has been simplified to exchanging contacts, and the deal is sealed.

With no iota of shame and second thought, women have stormed social media where they expose the true woman they are carrying in themselves. Using pictures, videos and text, posted on the internet, a greater content of which is outrageously immoral and denigrating to social norms, women proclaim their sexuality to the world more than history has ever known. They take advantage of the privacy of their computers to describe their sexual egos in complete detail and frankness; what they have not been able to whisper to the ears of any man, even those that they had pretended to confide to. Fully aware of this flirtatious character of women and girls, men have adopted a careful and vigilant approach in their love relationships.

One documented and apparently well researched complaint that men have so far made against women, was published in December 2009, by the blogger Reality2010. Women will not be at ease with the unequivocal and concise details given in the critic. According to Reality2010, all started to go wrong with women in the 1960s with the upshot of feminist movements. He said, "Like the Nazis blaming the Jews for their own failure, women sought to blame another group of people for their own inadequacies and failures and that was men... All it amounts to is that women were jealous of all the recognition men received for their accomplishments, which they too wanted, but without all the work."

Reality2010 pinches almost all sectors of women's life in his essay in which he blames public policy for its complicity with women's unjustified demands. According to him;

"Laws and government programs were introduced to 'level the playing field,' to try to compensate for women's incredible shortcomings in virtually every area of men's occupations. But all these new laws did was reward those who do nothing -women and punish those who work hard –men, by giving women artificial advantages over men." He explains that, women say that they "have come so far", but that, so much has been done for women who have done nothing.

Reality2010 believes that, feminism and its new laws have made women accountable to no one, "not to employers, not to their family or husbands, or even to the legal system…" To him, "Feminism shifted gears and started pushing a new 'agenda'. Women have been brainwashed by the contradicting edicts of mainstream feminism, they don't see that it all runs counter to their own best interests in living the natural life that is fulfilling to a woman. It isn't until women turn 40 that they begin to wake up and realize what idiots they have been all their lives."

Lambasting women, Reality2010 declares that women have never done anything of real significance and because they are unable to compete with men, feminism set about to lower the standards of 'achievement. Women of the upper class, he explains, who have the privilege of higher education, chose to lead frivolous and pointless lives.

Human sexuality according Reality2010 is at its lowest standard because of the attitude of women. He estimates that, 80 percent of the females are having sex with 20 percent of the powerful males in the society. And that, 85 percent of all women cheat on their husbands with no guilt at all, explaining why STD infection rates are astronomically higher amongst women "they are inadvertently sharing STD's with one another, and with the men they are sharing." Reality2010 warned that the men are ignorant of this lifestyle of women "It is astounding how very few people know this."

In a typical masculine style Reality2010 accuses women for being lazy "majority of women are not willing to make the sacrifice for demanding professions; most women simply do not have any interest in science, law, technology, or business." The modern female to him, "is tyrannical, confrontational and constantly complaining with no accountability but always criticizing and blaming everyone around them." He asserts that, the more educated a woman is, the more abusive she is, contrary to the man- the less educated a man is the more abusive he is.

Girls he says "learn the art of manipulating men at a very early age." The result to him is that, today's women are very crafty at getting what they want from men but have no corresponding intelligence or any real life skills. "Women who don't know anything are incredibly proud of it, like the woman who says, - I don't know if the world is flat or round, and I don't care…. After all, why on Earth would you want to learn electrical engineering or auto mechanics when you can have a man do it for you, or, why engage in any serious field of study for financial gain, when you can just exploit lonely men by obtaining their property through the divorce court industry, which constitutes legal fraud?"

On morals, Reality2010 claims that women feel that they are morally superior to men, so because, women are never held accountable for their actions. Women to him, blame everyone else around them for their own destructive actions in accusations like "you are responsible for my bad behavior! Even if I drink too much and go out with several men, it's all your fault; as my husband, it's your fault I cheated on you!"

In child upbringing, Reality2010 thinks that women make horrible decisions and abuse children far more than men because of their emotional instability. The consequence is the behavioral problems children of single mothers have today. He blames the society for making things easy for women and thereby compromising standards and quality, "providing women with a litany of entitlements, handouts, hiring preferences, flexible schedules, etc, and instead of improving, during the last 40 years, women have gradually invented their own separate world where what is considered 'accomplishment' has a completely alien definition."

It would be interesting to have our women respond to these very serious accusations made against them. It is true that men would find some real truth in the ideas of Reality2010. Some women attempt to justify these with the view that it is the woman's only options to be able to survive chronic male domination.

BIBLIOGRAPHY

ALCOFF, LINDA: The problem of speaking for others. Minnesota: University of Minnesota Press, 1991 Cultural Critique.

ROUSSEAU, JEAN-JACQUES: The Social Contract. Cambridge, U.K: Cambridge University Press, 1997.

PITKIN, HANNA: The Concept of Representation, Los Angeles: University Press, 1967.

STANFORD ENCYCLOPEDIA of Philosophy, 2014.

MILL, JOHN STUART: Considerations on Representative Government. Great Books of the Western World 43. Chicago: Encyclopaedia Britannica, 1952: Encyclopedia.com, 2014.

BURKE, EDMUND: Speech at Conclusion on the Polls, 3 November, 1774. In The Writings and speeches of Edmund Burke. Vol III: P, Parliament and the American War, 1774 - 1780. Oxford: Clarendon, 1989.

VON RAUTENFELD, HANS: Political Representation. New Dictionary of the History of Ideas. 2005. Encyclopedia.com. 17 June 2014.

MONTESQUIEU, CHARLES, in Von Rautenfeld Hans: Political Representation. New Dictionary of the History of Ideas. 2005. Encyclopedia.com. 17 June 2014.

MADISON, JAMES in: Political Representation. New Dictionary of the History of Ideas. 2005. Encyclopedia.com. 17 June 2014.

MANIN, BERNARD: The Principles of Representative Government, Cambridge: 7Cambridge University Press, 1997. In the Stanford Encyclopedia of Philosophy, 2014.

GOLDWIN, ROBERT & SCHAMBER, WILLIAM: How Democratic is the Constitution. Washington D.C: American Enterprise Institute, 1980.

DE BEAUVOIR, SIMONE: The Second Sex. First published as *Le Deuxième Sexe*, 1949; translated by H M Parshley, Penguin, 1972.

MODISE, THANDI : Chairperson of the National Council of Provinces, speech to Members of Parliament, Old Assembly, Parliament, 3 June 2014.

LOAT, ALISON & MACMILLAN, MICHAEL, Interview: A Call for Constituency Training. Post, October 15, 2014, Ardentmarbles. https://constituencytraining.wordpress.com/2014/10/15/interview

SALEEM, SADIA: from Moiz Amjad's commentary on Ghamidi's 'Manshur.' renaissance.com.pk/jauisma96.html. Dec. 2014.

DE LA BARRE, POULAIN in, Simone de Beauvoir: The Second Sex. translated by H M Parshley, Penguin, 1972.

COGHILL, KEN: 'How Should Elected Members Learn Parliamentary Skills?' Papers on Parliament, No. 59 April 2013 http://www.aph. gov.au/About_Parliament/Senate/Research_and_Education

BAN KI-MOON: United Nations Secretary General, speech on the International Day for the Girl Child, 2014

Interview: John Gerassi, 1976;Published: *Society*, Jan-Feb. 1976; Source: Southampton University; Proofed: and corrected by Andy Blunden, February 2005. Copyright: 1995 by Transaction Publishers.

Harmonistion of Children's Laws in Cameroon, published by The African Child Policy Forum.

VERMA, RAGINI: in How Men's Brains Are Wired Differently Than Women's by Tanya Lewis, Staff Writer December 02, 2013 http:// www.livescience.com/41619.

WANG, MASTER: in The Art of War by Sun Tzu p96. London, Oxford University Press, 1971.

NZILKOUE, CHRISTIAN: The Children's Parliament thrives in Central African Republic by Linda Tom ; UNICEF Connect, 18 Nov 2014 .

Children's Parliament Scotland: Giving ideas a voice; http://www. childrensparliament.org.uk/whats-in-a-name.html

BROWN GEORGE: in The Senate Of Canada. A Legislative and Historical Overview of the Senate of Canada, Committees and Private Legislation Directorate Revised May 2001. http://www.parl. gc.ca/About/Senate/LegisFocus/legislative-e.htm, Jan. 2015

ENCYCLOPEDIA BRITANNICA: http://www.britannica.com/ EBchecked/topic/348064/House-of-Lords

DUA, PRANAV: Essay on Problems of Women in Modern India. 2015 World's Largest Collection of Essays! Published by Experts. http://www.shareyouressays.com/87309/ essay-on-problems-of-women-in-modern-india

BACHELET, MICHELLE: in Evaluating Challenges Women Face; By Luisita Lopez Torregrosa. The New York Times, Published: March 6, 2012 The Female Factor. http://www.nytimes.com/2012/03/07/ us/07iht-letter07.html?

CALVERT, ROZ: in What Are Some Problems Women Face in Africa? eHow http://www.ehow.com/list_7415014_problems-women-face-africa_.htm

VALLELY, PAUL: From dawn to dust, the daily struggle of Africa's women. The Independent, September 2006.

REALITY2010: Blog, The Problem With Women Today, What in the Hell happened to women? Friday, December 4, 2009. http:// problemwithwomentoday.blogspot.com)

www.ingramcontent.com/pod-product-compliance
Lightning Source LLC
Chambersburg PA
CBHW020525290526
45786CB00002B/757